beyond expectations

beyond expectations

FINDING JOY

IN YOUR

MARRIAGE

NANCY SEBASTIAN MEYER

MOODY PUBLISHERS
CHICAGO

All Scripture quotations, unless otherwise indicated, are taken from the *Holy Bible, New International Version®*. NIV®. Copyright © 1973, 1978, 1984 by International Bible Society. Used by permission of Zondervan Publishing House. All rights reserved.

Scripture quotations marked KJV are taken from the King James Version.

Scripture quotations marked AMP are taken from the *Amplified Bible, Old Testament*, copyright © 1965, 1987 by The Zondervan Corporation. The *Amplified Bible, New Testament*, copyright © 1954, 1958, 1987 by The Lockman Foundation. Used by permission.

Scripture quotations marked NLT are taken from the *Holy Bible, New Living Translation*, copyright © 1996. Used by permission of Tyndale House Publishers, Inc., Wheaton, Illinois 60189. All rights reserved.

Library of Congress Cataloging-in-Publication Data

Meyer, Nancy Sebastian, 1961-
    Beyond expectations : finding joy in your marriage / Nancy Sebastian Meyer.
        p. cm.
    Includes bibliographical references (p.   ).
    ISBN 0-8024-1639-X
    I. Wives—Religious life. 2. Christian women—Religious life. 3. Marriage—Religious aspects—Christianity. I. Title.

BV4528.15.M49 2003
248.8'435—dc21

2002155777

1 3 5 7 9 10 8 6 4 2

Printed in the United States of America

To Rich, my husband.
You are God's choice for me,
and I love you.
Yesterday, today, and tomorrow—
whatever each day may hold.
You're the one.

To my precious daughter, Becky.
May you find joy
in your walk with God.
And in God's perfect time,
may He give you
your "Prince Charming"
to love and cherish.

To my prayer partners.
May God richly bless you for
your faithful, loving support,
which time and time again has borne me up
on the wings of prayer.

Contents

A Personal Note

Dear Reader:

A woman absolutely committed to the pursuit of a fulfilling marriage relationship has written the book you now hold. She has sustained this determination through the ups and downs, zigs and zags, and unforeseen convolutions of a challenging marriage.

I know this because I am her husband.

While contending with the obstacles and celebrating the triumphs within our relationship, Nancy has forged and proven principles for being a loving wife. She has energetically conveyed these to women individually and in groups and has more recently developed this book in order to reach you.

The principles presented in these pages can help marriages. Our relationship is proof of it.

Sincerely,
Rich Meyer

Preparing for the Journey

$\mathcal{S}$everal years ago, one of our favorite out-of-town couples came to visit us. That particular Saturday afternoon, our two-year-old took a nap while my friend and I sat down for a chat. Meanwhile, her husband cajoled Rich into working together on a building project in our basement.

Rich got so engrossed in his work that he forgot about his buddy on the other side of the wall. He bellowed to me a request to find his something or other. When I accidentally handed him the wrong tool, he responded with more than a little frustration.

When I returned to my friend, she asked me to follow her upstairs, where she asked me, "How long has he been talking to you like that?" The concern in her voice and on her face made me feel guilty and relieved. For the first time in what seemed like forever, someone heard my pain.

Rich's unkind words hurt me. My friend validated that hurt. She told me I wasn't being "too sensitive," and it was OK to feel bad about how he talked to me. She also told me I needed counseling. She was right, but it took me another eight to ten months of God's preparation of my heart before I accepted the help I needed.

This book offers you validation and help. Life, especially marriage, doesn't always turn out as we expect it will. We need to get "beyond expectations" and on to the life God is calling us to live with the spouse He has given us.

God walked me through the journey first, and now I'm here to walk it with you as I have with other wives who want more joy in their marriages.

This is perhaps the best time to give a word of warning. The following material is *not* intended for wives suffering in marriages that involve serious abuse, addictions, adultery, or desertion. A woman suffering in that type of situation needs the immediate help of a professional Christian counselor. Although many of the following chapters can potentially help her focus more clearly on God and see herself as whole and approved, she also needs to learn how to deal appropriately with the distinct problems in her marriage. Such a person might be tempted to use the truths in this book to try to live above a very real problem. As difficult as it may seem, the problem must be addressed and resolved for the sake of the marriage and both spouses. In this situation, *Beyond Expectations* may be a good book to come back to *after* resolving any major issues.

A Foundation of Essential Truths

To prepare you to get the most out of this book, I want to share with you what I believe are essential truths—so very important to your successful growth and progress. These points make up the strong foundation we will need throughout the book.

1. *God is.* If I didn't believe that everything starts and ends with God, I would be nothing but a most miserable creature. And this book could not exist. Every truth you read comes from the Word of God or is represented in His perfect character. Although I may cite or refer to

other sources, all truth belongs to God. I believe in Him with every fiber of my being. If you do not believe in Him, ask God to reveal Himself and His truth to you. For you cannot fully benefit from the truths in this book unless you accept them as they are . . . from God.

2. *God can be trusted.* An elderly widow and widower in my church got married several years ago. For each anniversary, the gentleman plans a "mystery trip" for his bride. He has taken her to Hawaii, England, and Australia. She never knows where they are going before they reach their destination. She only receives little hints on what type of clothing to pack and how many days they'll be gone. Although this may sound delightful, her situation demands complete trust in her husband. She knows his character. He is kind, thoughtful, and generous. She knows his past record full of incredibly wonderful surprises. And so she trusts him and goes wherever he takes her. Can you trust God, even if He doesn't show you more than the very next step? Can you say these words: *"I'm Yours, Lord. Take me wherever I need to go, through whatever is necessary to become the person You want me to be."*

3. *God's Word is our best source of truth.* Although most of this book is written in my own words, the Word of God is the ultimate source of truth in any and every situation. My words are merely the vehicle to get you to the truth of God's Word. Often throughout this book we will refer to and analyze passages of Scripture that have the ability to bring clarity and change to our lives. I hope you will open your Bible and read God's words for yourself, even though many verses will be printed within the text of this book. "I wait for the LORD, my soul waits, and in his word I put my hope" (Psalm 130:5).

4. *God has promised to be with us now and forever.* Even though God doesn't wear skin or speak audibly or hold you in a human embrace, He is with you—every day, everywhere you may go. His Word tells us we can never get away from Him, once we acknowledge our need for a Savior and invite Him into our lives to take His rightful place as Lord. In verses 7 through 10 of Psalm 139, David speaks of God's presence

with us. "Where can I go from your Spirit? Where can I flee from your presence? If I go up to the heavens, you are there; if I make my bed in the depths, you are there. If I rise on the wings of the dawn, if I settle on the far side of the sea, even there your hand will guide me, your right hand will hold me fast." Indeed, God promised, "Never will I leave you; never will I forsake you" (Hebrews 13:5).

5. *An important part of owning these truths is journaling.* I am not, by nature, a journaler. I find it cumbersome and painstakingly slow to put my feelings and thoughts of the moment down on paper. However, when I really need to think something through and practice the truth I'm learning, the best method for remembering is to write down (or type into the computer, make a chart, etc.) whatever truth and application I want to put into practice. And putting a lesson into practice helps to establish it in my mind. If you are truly serious about wanting change in your life, I encourage you to keep a pen and journal handy as you read this book. Perhaps at the end of each chapter, you will write down the main truths presented, how those truths affect your life, and what you are going to do about them.

6. *You cannot change anyone but yourself.* Until a few years ago I seriously thought I could change my husband. I even figured I had an obligation to help him get over all of his faults. How silly that sounds now. The truth is we have no power to change anyone but ourselves. God isn't asking us to change someone else. Yes, you can pray for your husband. And you may even be able to influence him by your words, actions, or reactions. But only he and God have the power to change him. And God has an advantage over both of you, because He is the God of the impossible. In Mark 9:23, Jesus said to a man, "Everything is possible for him who believes." The man responded, "I do believe; help me overcome my unbelief!" Will you pray these words to our heavenly Father right now? Ask Him to help you remember whom you can change. With God's help you can become the kind of woman and wife in whom He delights. You can also learn that your husband is in God's hands and find rest and hope in that fact.

7. *There is always hope.* Because of God, there is always hope . . . even in hopeless situations, even with hopeless people. I am well aware that the truths in this book cannot directly change your husband's life or your situation just because you read these words. I can, however, guarantee that the God of this book always offers hope in every situation. The hope God offers is on His terms and is not often what we might choose for ourselves. But His way is always best. Hope is always offered. And God's hope never disappoints. At a particular time in the lives of the Old Testament Jews, when they faced unbelievable and incredibly terrifying circumstances, Jeremiah recorded these words from God. "'For I know the plans I have for you,' declares the LORD, 'plans to prosper you and not to harm you, plans to give you hope and a future'" (Jeremiah 29:11). God offers you the same promise today: a promise of hope for the journey to tomorrow.

A PREVIEW OF OUR JOURNEY

This journey, based upon a secure foundation of truth, includes the following sections.

Part One: Once Upon a Time. Come, hear my story. Add to this the stories of five other fictitious-based-on-fact couples. Can you relate to one or more of the women? Look at your own marriage and see the connections.

Part Two: Looking Inside. Open the door to your marriage and take a look inside. Identify the expectations you carried with you down the aisle to your waiting groom. Examine what has transpired since then—both positive and negative. Look into the future and dream again . . . with a godly perspective. We'll also take some time to examine who you are, what qualities your husband possesses, and how you can work together instead of against each other. Perhaps for the very first time you will feel a freedom to be the very special, precious person God originally designed.

Part Three: Getting Real. Do you remember the story *The Velveteen Rabbit?* A child's stuffed bunny learns that becoming "real" means being loved so hard and long that "most of your hair has been loved off, and your eyes drop out and you get loose in the joints and very shabby." The story goes on, "But these things don't matter at all, because once you are Real you can't be ugly, except to people who don't understand." Once you get real with God, once you really connect with Him on His terms, you will never be the same. Life will be entirely new to you. New and full of hope.

Part Four: Independence and Dependence. Most women who come to my classes or sit across the kitchen counter and tell me about unhappy marriages are needy women. Do you feel unfulfilled and unsatisfied in your marriage? You probably have many needs which have never even occurred to your husband. Where and how can you go about getting your needs met? Complete and satisfied, you can joyfully and purposefully begin to spill over into the lives of those around you— most importantly your husband.

Part Five: Dealing with the Past. We will walk through your deserts of disappointment, despair, and devastation. Would you like to be free from the burden of past pain, sin, guilt, bitterness, and anger? You can get through and over to the other side. God's Word and His Spirit will be our comfort, strength, and hope. "God did not give us a spirit of timidity, but a spirit of power, of love and of self-discipline" (2 Timothy 1:7). I like the term the King James Version of the Bible uses instead of self-discipline: "a sound mind." So, do not fear. By God's promise, we shall walk through past pain with power, love, and a sound mind.

Part Six: The Power of Healing Words. How do you communicate healing to your husband? Here we will begin the process of learning and applying the principles of being positive, respectful, and assertive. Many women in my classes have reported that their husbands actually begin to change at this stage of the journey. Imagine that! God is doing great things in His children's marriages.

Part Seven: Intimacy Renewed. By this point in the book you are hopefully on your way to becoming "mature and complete, not lacking anything" (James 1:4) and ready to give to your husband out of an emotionally full tank. You are ready to become his friend once again. And his lover. Oh, the joy of falling in love . . . again!

When all of life is boiled down, where is my focus? Why am I here? What is my ultimate goal? The true answer to these questions is what keeps us going . . . what gives us enduring hope . . . God Himself. Come, travel with me to the end of our journey—and the beginning of true joy in marriage and in every other part of life.

A FINAL WORD ON PRAYER

A final word on your preparation for the journey. Pray. This book is only a tool to guide you on the journey. The author is only a messenger of the real Guide. God Himself is ready to make the trip with you. Remember to walk each step with Him. Talk to Him about everything, anytime, all of the time.

The value of talking to God (praying) comes in four forms: comfort, confidence, compassion, and character. Praying means we've crawled up on our heavenly Father's lap, snuggled in, and are talking to Him about what is on our hearts—that's real comfort. There is no one bigger or stronger or more able to take care of my concerns—I have confidence in Him. When I pray over and over for another person, God grants me a supernatural compassion (love) for him or her—and I need God's love for my husband when my own love runs short. And over time, praying through times of suffering produces "perseverance; perseverance, character; and character, hope. And hope does not disappoint us, because God has poured out his love into our hearts by the Holy Spirit, whom he has given us" (Romans 5:3–5).

So pray. Praise God, repent of your sins, ask for what you need, and yield your heart and life to God every day. "Do not be anxious about anything, but in everything, by prayer and petition, with thanksgiving, present your requests to God. And the peace of God, which transcends all understanding, will guard your hearts and your minds in Christ Jesus" (Philippians 4:6–7).

Especially pray for your husband. Let me urge you to get your Bible and read Colossians 1:9–14. This is an excellent prayer to pray for your husband on a regular basis. Instead of praying (as we all naturally tend to do), "God please help him to (fill in the blank), and please fix (fill in the blank) and (fill in the blank) . . . ," try praying the following prayer, adapted from the Colossians passage.

> *Dear God, thank You for my husband. Please grant him knowledge of You and Your will, spiritual wisdom and understanding, a life that pleases You and brings You glory, spiritual fruit and good works, strength, endurance, and appreciation for who he is (or can be) in You. Thank You for the joy we've shared. Thank You for the hope we have in You. Thank You for what You are going to do in me to make me a better wife for him. Thank You for my husband. I love You, Lord.*

Know that I am praying for you, dear reader, as you embark on this journey of hope and renewal. God will take you Beyond Expectations to a new joy in your marriage. "Now to him who is able to do immeasurably more than all we ask or imagine, according to his power that is at work within us, to him be glory in the church and in Christ Jesus throughout all generations, for ever and ever! Amen" (Ephesians 3:20–21).

Once Upon
a Time

Dear Father God,

My fairy tale is crumbling.

Life hasn't turned out as I hoped.

No one else seems to understand.

Help!

I punched the garage-door opener and twisted the key in the ignition with a vengeance. Trying to swallow the lump in my throat, I impatiently waited for the door to clear my exit. *Why bother with a seat belt? If anything happens to me, I wouldn't be missed.*

I jerked backward into the inky night, hit the remote button by habit to lower the garage door, and squealed my tires in a frantic rush to leave the house—and the conflicts with my husband. He always won every disagreement. I always caved in, eventually finding myself at the same point. "OK, it's my fault. I'm a jerk," I'd say, playing the part of the victim. And on very rare occasions I'd run away—not for long, not far.

Complying with the stop sign at the end of our quiet street, I sat trembling, with tears running down my cheeks and my hands clenching the steering wheel. Where could I go? Names of people ran through my mind. But at eleven o'clock at night, I could think of no one who would be interested in taking me in, let alone know what to do with me. After all, a women's Sunday school teacher is supposed to have it all together. *Yeah, like her marriage!* Did I really want anyone to see me like this? Did I want to reveal how horrible my marriage had become—how frustrated and trapped I felt?

I'd been down this road before—literally. When everything caved in on me, I'd tried to run away once or twice. But I never got farther than this stop sign. Not more than one sensible alternative existed. I married the man; now I had to live with him. I tried to rationalize with myself. *He's really not so awful. As a matter of fact, the problems in the marriage aren't all his fault. True, he's hard to please. But that's a big part of my problem. I promise more than I can follow through on. He's never satisfied. I'm always wrong.* I took a deep breath and sighed.

I thought back a few minutes to our heated discussion. Rich was angry with me for umpteen reasons, some spoken, others just hanging in the air between us. *I can't live like this anymore. I can't do anything to please him. Something's always wrong.* I rested my head on the steering wheel. *He clearly doesn't need me . . . with all my weaknesses and problems. Somebody else, with more consistency, would do a much better job washing his laundry, cooking his meals, and cleaning his house. He'd just be better off without me.* Another thought hit me. *Our insurance policy is paid up, isn't it?*

But, Becky . . . Our six-year-old, sleeping in her little bed, was totally oblivious to my shattered world. I wanted my little sweetheart to have the best in life. She, too, needed someone with consistency. What kind of mother would she have if I died and Rich remarried? *She'd get over it eventually if something happened to me. Grandma and Grandpa would help. They live just down the street.*

I looked out my car window at their house . . . the home where I'd grown up. Mom and Dad were probably inside right now watching the news, also oblivious to the depth of pain I was experiencing. I had always tried not to tell them too much. They would be so sad. I was their only child. Fresh tears ran down my cheeks. They would be so disappointed with me if they knew.

Talk about disappointment! Since an early age, my three life goals consisted of becoming a pastor's wife, teaching kindergarten, and raising twelve kids. I married a youth pastor, but he was now in the business world. I taught school for several years, but never kindergarten. And we only had one child—with little hope for any more. Furthermore, marriage was as different from my fairy tale dream of "happily ever after" as a lazy summer afternoon is to a cold winter's night. Life looked pretty bleak.

I looked at the stars through my tears. "God, are You sure You don't want me in heaven right now? I'm willing to come. My marriage is a mess. I can't stand Rich, and I'm not so sure I even like myself. Please take me home." A quietness settled over me.

How long had I been sitting at the stop sign? Because traffic was virtually nonexistent at this time of night, I had not been forced to move. But I had to go somewhere. Only one solution agreed with everything I knew and believed. I had to go home. I was needed. God would work things out. *Yeah, right,* I thought with a remnant of bitterness. *And look how far that philosophy has gotten you so far.*

I dug a tissue out of the glove box, blew my nose, and wiped my face. The initial signs of anxiety had left my body. My breathing had slowed down, my face didn't feel quite so overheated, and I'd finally stopped shaking. The tension wasn't gone, but it was better. I took another deep breath. Leaving home wasn't a good solution—I really didn't want to go somewhere else. I wanted to stay right here. What I really wanted was for my husband to change. *Why couldn't we like each other like we used to?* His angry words and noticeable disapproval and disappointment just weren't things I wanted to live with for the rest of my life.

"God, I'm gonna need Your help here." I put the car into gear and slowly turned around in a neighbor's driveway. I needed to go where God was calling me to do His work. In my home. With my husband. With my child.

As I turned into our driveway, I hit the remote again and watched the door go up. Once in the garage, I parked the car, climbed out, and closed the garage door. I walked into the darkened kitchen. Rich had gone to bed. Becky had been in her bed for almost three hours already. I put my elbows on the countertop, and I propped my head in my hands. "God, where do I go from here?"

To bed, child. Rest in Me. I am the One who loves you, approves of you, and accepts you just as you are, My forgiven child. Rest now, little one.

I yawned and headed to bed.

DISAPPOINTING AND DISAPPOINTED

In the first twelve years of our marriage, I was disappointed—and I was a disappointment. I learned that disappointment stems from unfulfilled expectations. My husband wasn't the prince I'd expected, and I was not able to fulfill Rich's expectations. Living up to the image of the godly wife I'd dreamed of being seemed impossible. Of course, our relationship didn't begin this way—what marriage does?

At Lancaster Bible College, I met and fell in love with my own personal Prince Charming. Our differences numbered as grains of sand on a beach. Rich came from Long Island, New York, and thrived on the concept of ministering in a metropolis (such as New York City). I grew up in Lancaster County, Pennsylvania, surrounded by Amish farms, and I loved the quiet country life. My studies in elementary education fit my vision to teach school and minister in a small Lancaster County Christian school. Rich was a strong leader; I happily followed along. I talked a hundred miles a minute, and he listened. (He knew how much I talked *before* he married me—but, to adapt a phrase, "love is deaf!")

We waited until just one week after graduation to tie the knot. The day I married Rich Meyer, I saw him as everything I wanted in a husband—or at least, I reasoned, with the potential to become what I wanted him to be. Rich was called to the youth pastorate. And I, happily, felt called to be his helpmate. He was a strong, passionate, godly leader. Our talents, abilities, and spiritual gifts matched and complemented each other's. And he knew just how to make me feel w-o-n-d-e-r-f-u-l. I'd never met anyone else quite like him. We were certain that God created us for each other.

After the wedding, we began our ministry together in a church just a little over an hour from Lancaster. After the bliss of dating and courtship, the first annoying incidents that cropped up were rather easy to ignore. Growing pains. Little adjustments, I told myself. I forgave easily and continued on. To be totally honest, I'd have to say that Rich overlooked his share of problems with me, as well. There were funny problems —the kind that you can laugh at later—like the time I burned cookies and set off the smoke alarm, and disconnected the battery but did not realize the alarm had to be unplugged as well. But there were also irritations, grudges, and mean words. We lived and learned.

Little things that bothered us about each other gradually intensified. After all, you can forgive a person when he does something you don't like once, even two or three times. But the nineteenth time it happens you wonder if he is really trying to change or if he doesn't care how you feel about it.

After two years of serving as a youth pastor in the first church, Rich and I moved on and spent another two years in a different church's youth department. Toward the end of this time, we took the youth group on a retreat. After we returned home from the event and saw the teens safely to their homes, Rich instructed me to take him to the emergency room of the local hospital. The emergency technicians confirmed a serious vertebrae problem in his back that would need immediate surgery the next day. I remember leaving the hospital in tears, wondering how I'd be able to sleep without him—we'd never been apart overnight since our wedding. I consoled myself with a soft shirt of Rich's I found in the laundry basket. It smelled like him, and I finally fell asleep with my arms wrapped around it. The whole incident helped put my petty irritations with my husband back into perspective . . . for a time.

Very soon after Rich came home from the hospital, the elders of our church came to visit him. He announced, to everyone's astonishment (including mine), that he had given much thought to the fact that he was not meeting the church's expectations. On the other hand, he explained, church work was not challenging him to 100 percent of what he considered his "career potential." He announced we were leaving the church, effective immediately.

This change eventually brought us back to Lancaster, where Rich became the assistant to the president of a publishing company. After another two years, he joined my father in the family photography business. This new endeavor didn't work out as well as everyone anticipated, and he left after yet another two years and went into the truck-driving profession. Yes, trucking—as in eighteen-wheelers that scream across America from coast to coast. After two years of driving, hauling, and loading, a second emergency back problem returned him to the hospital. Rich's next two years were spent *at home* living on workmen's compensation, in a state of understandably low self-esteem and "nothing to show" for the ten years since his college graduation.

I'm sure you've picked up the pattern. I call Rich my "two-year wonder," simply because every two years I wonder what new career or job he's going to try next. But why tell you all about my husband? Because I'm sure you are beginning to feel just by reading these events some of the emotions, changes, insecurities, worries, and fear I experienced as his wife. Let me detail one more component in our situation that perhaps dwarfs the others by its sheer magnitude.

THE BIG SHOCK

One eventful Sunday morning, during the time Rich was working with my dad and Becky was almost a year old, my husband walked into the kitchen in jeans—not our normal church attire. He got right to the point. "My prayers are hitting the ceiling. I can't feel God. I can't see God."

I remember standing completely still, in a state of shock in which I was intently aware of everything. The clock ticked loudly. The Formica felt cool to my fingertips. I could just catch the scent of Rich's aftershave. *This can't be happening to me.* I wondered if I'd said the words aloud. A buzzing in my head grew so loud it almost drowned out Rich's next words.

"I can't go to church week after week and sit there like a hypocrite." He looked sad. "I need some time and some space to sort this out. I'm not going to go to church with you for a while. I'm sorry."

I don't remember what we ate for breakfast or what the pastor preached about that morning. I probably looked like the walking dead. I didn't know what to say to people, even weeks and months later. And sitting in church without my husband caused some of the loneliest times I've ever experienced.

I'm sorry to say that for many, many months I was so devastated and disappointed about how this situation affected *my* life, I didn't give much thought and even less prayer to Rich's very real spiritual needs. Very often quiet about his inner thoughts and feelings, he said little about his spiritual journey—or lack thereof. I find it hard to admit, but I spent much time being selfishly annoyed because Rich wasn't following the story line I'd prepared for our fairy-tale marriage.

Over the next couple of years I walked through the stages of grief—grief over the loss of our spiritual oneness. Finally, Scripture passages, prayer, and counsel from friends brought me around to a much more godly perspective on myself and my marriage. In the midst of some of the greatest pain, I remember someone saying, "Nancy, you have a choice. You can be better or bitter. Only one letter makes all the difference in the world." I decided to choose "better"—by God's grace. Truly, even through times of frustration and disappointment, anger and tears, disillusionment and despair, God has faithfully walked with me and worked on me, teaching me precious truths.

I also began to pray fervently that Rich would see God and love Him again with his whole heart. At a point of total surrender, I gave myself, Rich, Becky, our home, our health, and all our valuables into God's hands—giving over whatever He needed to take or touch to bring Rich back to Himself.

As callous as it may seem, I actually rejoiced when Rich's second back injury rendered him temporarily paralyzed, because I saw it as God's way of getting his attention. I was sure God was speaking to him in a way he would understand and bringing him back to the truth. But in fact, Rich's spiritual disposition changed very little. And the following two years at home in rehabilitation were worse for our marriage than anything else to that point. Nothing satisfied him . . . especially not me.

During this difficult time, I developed the opinion that I needed to be as perfect as possible. I'll bet you've been here a time or two yourself. First, I figured if I did everything right, Rich wouldn't have anything to complain about, which would alleviate conflict. Second, I must reflect

Christ because I was the Christian to whom he was most exposed. If he saw Christ in me, he might be moved closer to God. If I goofed up, I was sure I'd push him even farther away.

But I couldn't accomplish perfection. My unrealistic and then failed expectations for myself left me in a constant state of guilt. Ready to burst into a million pieces, I called our pastor of counseling and made an appointment. After that first session, I went home and told Rich what I'd done.

"I went to see Jay Diller today. He's the counseling pastor at church. I think you'd like him." I held up my hand to stop him from interrupting. "No, I'm not asking you to go to counseling with me. I know that you aren't happy with me." I took a deep breath. "The point is . . . I've realized I can't change you, but I can change me. And I'm willing to try to change the things you don't like about me for the sake of our marriage." Whew! I'd said it. After a pause I went on. "I think Jay can help me. But he needs to know what you don't like." I suggested Rich could make a list I could take with me to the next appointment. But he chose to go along with me just for that one session.

I realized a great sense of safety in Jay's office with Rich that day. This safety overwhelmed me, because I never before realized I feared my husband. Physical safety was not the issue, but words can hurt every bit as much as a physical blow. There in Jay's office, Rich and I found ourselves really communicating on some tough issues, with the benefit of a third party. We both realized our vast differences were keeping us from fully appreciating the other person. I think we also understood we both shared responsibility for the tension in our marriage.

Probably because of his own self-sufficiency, Rich didn't go back to see Jay for any personal benefit. But he did join me again some five or six months later at my last appointment. He acknowledged the improvements in my life, though he credited them to Jay, not God. Truly, after my talking, listening, reading books, and redirecting my perspective to God's view on me and my situation, I was once again the woman he fell in love with.

But the effects were somewhat short-lived. One year later, my heart felt stung when Rich suggested I go back and see Jay for a refresher. But he was right. I needed to reexamine my thinking against what I'd learned a year before. Isn't it amazing how quickly we revert to our old ways of thinking if we don't faithfully practice the truth? I sat down with my old notes. As I read those papers, my perspective almost immediately shifted back to God's truth. I was beginning to understand that I will never be "fixed." I will just keep learning and correcting things along the way until I see Jesus face-to-face.

PASSING ON WHAT I'VE LEARNED

It wasn't long before I was sharing the lessons I'd learned with other hurting wives. With an undergraduate degree in Bible and a master's in elementary education along with my marital experiences, I soon recognized God's call to teach and encourage Christian wives and women. My life gained renewed purpose.

Today my marriage is very different because I am different. God moved me from discontentment to a state of peace, from zero love for Rich back to 100 percent. God restored my hope, which is what I offer today: hope for the heart of any woman struggling with disappointments in her marriage—from small irritations to huge sins and hurts.

You can change. *But,* you may be saying to yourself, *it's not me that needs changing—it's my husband. He's the one with the problems.* Reality says that if your husband has problems, you've got them too. "We're all in this together" is one of Rich's phrases for our family. I, too, didn't want to take responsibility at first. But I finally realized an important fact: I can change no one but myself. So I decided to do what I could with what was available to me. Indeed, you and your marriage can change too. Change may not happen in just the way you expect or even desire. But change, God's way, is possible. Your husband may even change in the process.

You wouldn't be reading this right now unless you were looking for this kind of hope. And I can personally guarantee your hope is not misplaced. God changed my life, even after I was a Christian for twenty years. I'm still learning and growing every day. Furthermore, I now watch Him change the lives of troubled wives who come to my classes, "Hope for the Heart of a Wife."

You need to know that what I'm talking about in the rest of this book is not merely a bunch of good ideas. God's truth is alive and active. *He* is very much alive and active! Christianity is not a religion, but a relationship. And through that relationship, we gain freedom, unconditional love, complete acceptance, unlimited grace . . . everything we need to be "mature and complete, not lacking anything" (James 1:4b).

Am I happily married to a committed Christian pastor at this moment? We are much more happily married than we used to be. Rich feels more fulfilled since earning his masters degree in business administration from Penn State University and working in the field of human resources. His coworkers respect and appreciate his business savvy and giant heart. But so far, Rich still considers himself to be an agnostic—someone who doesn't believe a person can really know whether there is a God or not, and if He *is* real, he can't relate to Him.

So why does he allow me to share *our* story with you? Because he witnessed the changes in my life that came about due to what I want to share with you. He admits he's difficult to live with. And he believes in the sanctity of marriage. His original sentiment to me went something like this: "If you can help women stay in difficult marriages for the sake of the marriage and the children, go ahead and share what you need to." Perhaps he would not consider his attitude and continual support a miracle, but I do.

I have been to the pit and back. No, marriage is not always blissful. As strong-willed, stubborn, sometimes obstinate characters, Rich and I still "butt heads." But I now live a victorious Christian life because of what God is teaching me. Can you, too? A resounding *yes!*

Before we embark on our journey of hope and healing, I want you to realize you're not alone. In the next chapter you will meet Angie, Meghan, Carla, Polly, and Wendy—five other wives who are struggling in their marriages. These characters are not real-life people, but fictitious composites of the many women I've listened to and encouraged over the past years. The stories will sound believable, because we've all "been there, done that" to one degree or another. We struggle with the same types of issues, frustrations, and sin. These five women will take the journey with us throughout the book. Take heart, there is hope—for all of us! God can meet our needs. He can repair our hearts, restore our joy, and rekindle our marital love.

> *Dear God,*
> *Thank You for hope. Forgive my doubts and increase my faith as we journey together.*

2

Shattered Expectations

ANGIE AND NICK'S STORY

*A*ngie handed several papers to a woman sitting in a lawn chair waiting for the girls' soccer game to start. She used her other hand to shade her eyes from the setting sun. "Hi, I'm Angie, the coach's wife. Here's the roster with the girls' names, addresses, and phone numbers. And the other sheet is a list of the home and away games, as well as directions to other fields."

"Thanks. I'm Pam." She smiled and took the papers. "Does the coach's wife always get stuck with the paperwork?"

"Yeah, comes with the turf." Angie returned Pam's smile.

They groaned in unison. "No pun intended." Angie

giggled and plopped in the grass beside Pam's chair. "Whew. It's been a long day. The papers are handed out, so now I can enjoy the game."

"The kids are doing really great this year." As Pam gestured toward the girls in the field, a Bible and some papers began sliding off her lap. Both women reached for them at the same time.

"Hey, this looks interesting. Are you teaching a class?" Angie handed Pam the outline that had fallen to the grass between them.

"These notes are from a recent meeting I attended on marriage. I thought I'd review them while the girls warm up."

Angie looked out at the field. "Did you learn anything interesting?"

She tried hard not to sound too interested or give away the fact that her own marriage frustrated her.

As Pam told her briefly about being married to a man who lacked her commitment to God, Angie felt a real connection with her and identified with much of what she described. In fact, her throat felt thick with emotion, and she needed to blink rapidly to keep the tears back.

When Pam fell silent, Angie spoke in a soft voice. "Your husband sounds a lot like Nick. He decided a few years back he wasn't going to go to church anymore. It's so hard to get to church on a Sunday morning with three kids and no help. . . ." Her voice trailed off, and she picked a tall piece of grass. "I know I should go. But I'm not as strong as you are."

"I wasn't strong in the beginning, either. I cried a lot. If my mother hadn't been right down the street and offered to pick up the kids and me on Sunday mornings, I might have been tempted to give up too."

Angie rolled the blade of grass between her fingers as she stared out at the field. "I've almost given up." She sighed. "Nick's a really great guy—everybody loves him. But he's so different from the man I thought I married. Does that sound weird?"

"Not a bit. I hear it all the time." Pam grinned at her amazed expression. "Don't you wonder if we are everything they expected *us* to be?"

Angie's smile didn't quite reach her eyes. "I thought I'd be the one to handle the checkbook and bills, but he wants to do it. And we never seem to have enough money to do the things I'd really like to do—like a family vacation. My family always went on vacation together every summer. We've been married fourteen years and have yet to take a real vacation.

Sometimes the kids and I go with my parents to the beach for a weekend." She sighed and absently twirled the piece of grass. "We shop differently. I like to buy in bulk and use coupons. He spends money spontaneously, and then clamps down if we seem to be running short."

"Do you ever talk about money and family spending?"

Angie looked appalled at the very thought of discussing her feelings with her husband. She shook her head. "I'm sorry. I shouldn't be loading you down with all this. You'll never talk with me at a soccer game again."

Pam waved her hand to dismiss the need for an apology. "Sometimes it's easier to talk things out with a third party." She smiled. "Especially someone who will listen and pray for you."

As Angie gratefully hugged her new friend, the referee blew his whistle, and the two women turned their attention to their daughters' soccer game.

MEGHAN AND KEITH'S STORY

Meghan slid into the pew just as the organ prelude began. With a sigh of relief from getting everyone to their destinations on time this particular Sunday morning, she dropped her purse on the floor and propped her Bible in the hymn rack. After bowing her head briefly to confess her worry and fretting, she glanced at the person beside her.

"Oh, hi, Shirley!" She chuckled softly, keeping her voice to a whisper. "I wasn't paying attention to where I was sitting when I plunked myself down. I haven't seen you for a while."

Shirley grinned back and replied just as quietly. "I figured you'd notice me soon enough. How've you been?"

Meghan wrinkled her nose and shook her head slightly. "Don't ask. I've been as fussy and picky with the kids lately as Keith usually is."

Shirley patted her hand. "I'm sure you're not being as hard on them as it seems. You're certainly more tenderhearted than Keith. Just be honest with the kids if you catch yourself overreacting, and apologize."

Meghan sighed and smiled. "You're so good for me."

"By the way, you look beautiful today. I love that color on you." Shirley touched the shiny, electric blue material of Meghan's skirt.

"You're *so* good for me." Meghan closed her eyes and savored the compliment. In a heartbeat, she was frowning. "I am so fat. I can't believe how much weight I've put on since high school." She rolled her eyes. "My twenty-five-year reunion's coming up in four months."

Shirley chuckled and sympathized that her class had celebrated number twenty the previous year.

Meghan put a hand on her stomach and whispered. "I'm embarrassed any more even to let Keith hug me. And he's been pretty critical lately. This fat is so gross, I know he hates the way I look. But the more I worry about it, the more I seem to eat." She grimaced. "How'd we get on this topic, anyway? The service is about to start. We'd better behave." She knew her grin and attempt at humor were a ruse to cover the depth of her frustration with herself and her husband.

CARLA AND PHIL'S STORY

"I just can't get Phil to talk to me. I know he thinks we should send Timmy to our local elementary school next year, but I want him to go to a Christian school. We need to talk about it." Carla's mouth turned down slightly at the corners before she bit into her chicken-salad sandwich. Her crisp, linen suit and the polished leather briefcase beside her chair told everyone at the restaurant she was on a lunch hour. Her friend Maria's casual appearance in jeans and a sweatshirt let them know this was certainly not a business meeting.

Carla dabbed her mouth with a napkin and continued her list of complaints. "He hardly talks to me at all. Does your husband talk much at home?" When her friend shrugged, she continued. "Well, Phil just wants to come in the door, plop on the couch, and watch television or read the paper—or both." She rolled her eyes as she speared a piece of lettuce and bite of tomato with her fork. "I can talk till I'm blue in the face, and I rarely get any response from the man. He seems happy enough to let me make all the decisions and run our home. I wish he'd take some ownership in this marriage."

"What kinds of things do you enjoy doing together?" Maria signaled the waitress with a request for more iced tea. "Do you do anything without Timmy—you know, like a date?"

Carla shook her head and frowned. "What fun would that be . . . with Mr. Boring? Besides, when would we find the time? Phil's job at the machine shop keeps him busy until six most evenings and sometimes on Saturday. My job's not as bad—at least I can bring work home." She fiddled with the chips on her plate, not making eye contact with Maria. "There's Timmy, too. He needs all my attention when I can be with him."

"Yeah, but Timmy will grow up and get a life of his own. You're stuck with Phil. Don't you think you ought to spend some quality time with *him*? Think of the reasons you married Phil. What did you like about him back then?" Maria smiled at Carla's thoughtful expression, slightly softening her facial features.

"Because he was . . ." Carla stared over her friend's shoulder into space, looking for distant memories. ". . . so handsome. And he was easy to hang out with. He loved to listen to my crazy stories. He was always there for me." She smiled. "He'd hold my hand or sit with his arm around me and tell me to relax and take a break. He was always so proud of me and the things I accomplished." Her eyes dulled, and her voice lowered to almost a whisper. "Now he doesn't even seem to notice me. I got a raise and he didn't say a word."

Maria cleared her throat and ventured a quiet guess. "You're making more than he is now?"

Carla flipped her hair behind her ear. "Yes, but he could be making more than he is with a little more initiative."

Maria changed the topic. "How's Timmy doing? Is he still spending the days with Phil's mom?"

"Yes." Carla paused, as if searching for the right words. "She's a dear, but she coddles him. Then she says I'm too hard on him. Somebody's gotta teach him to tow the line. He's got to be ready for kindergarten next year." She sighed and refolded her napkin alongside her plate. "Sorry I'm such a spoilsport today. Tell me about you. What's happening?"

They continued to talk another ten minutes or so. When the waitress left the check, Carla scooped it up, always in control of the situation. She never allowed Maria to pay for their lunches, "because I'm the working girl," she'd always say. She knew Maria had learned not to argue. *Funny, she thought, I wonder if maybe Phil has learned the same thing.*

As the two friends prepared to go their separate ways, Carla leaned close and said, "Pray for us, will you?"

POLLY AND KURT'S STORY

Polly tried to swallow her tears and calm down as she dialed her friend's phone number.

Ann picked up the phone on the second ring. "Hello, Jacksons'."

"It's me . . . Polly. I'm so . . . (hiccup) . . . frustrated." Polly's voice broke, and she stopped to clear her throat.

"Kurt just got home from work and immediately went out running. Dinner is ready, but he said he needed to run. Can you please pray for me? I need patience. I'm so mad." Sobs choked her voice.

"Polly, why don't you turn on a praise tape and listen to it as you feed the kids. Then clean up the kitchen and keep listening to the tape. Let the words flood your mind."

Polly sniffed. "I hate this. I feel like I'm in a giant pit, and when I try to climb out, Kurt just keeps knocking me down and throwing dirt on me."

"Let me pray with you right now." Ann began to pray aloud into the receiver. "Please lift Polly out of this pit and help her see this situation from Your viewpoint. Help her find something to rejoice in. In Jesus' name, amen."

"Thanks, Ann. I'll put in a tape right now and then feed the kids. Keep praying, will you?"

"You bet. Call me later if you want to."

After they hung up, Ann sat by her phone and remembered back to the days when Polly and Kurt first met. Kurt, a product of a prominent business family, inherited his father's forthright dealing savvy and his mother's winning ways. Then he'd fallen in love with quiet, practical Polly. She complemented his outgoing personality with her quiet, peaceful disposition. She organized his perpetual state of confusion. She never said anything wrong in a group of people . . . because she hardly ever said anything. And they were a very handsome couple.

Several years and five children later, Polly stayed at home rearing the children, while Kurt wheeled and dealt in the many family businesses, both local and abroad. Where their lives seemed magnificently successful, their marriage was not. Their differences escalated over the years and spread them even further apart from each other.

A remarkable homemaker, Polly made the Proverbs 31 woman look lazy. Her children were dressed well, her house was spotless (of course, Kurt insisted that with such a big house they needed a weekly cleaning lady), and she loved inviting friends over for lunch or a swim in the pool.

For the most part, no one saw the tiffs between Polly and Kurt. She had accepted the fact that disagreements are a given in marriage. She just couldn't get over the *way* Kurt argued with her. Fast and furious, the fights were always picked and won by Kurt. While he thrived on heated debates and competition, Polly shied away from any and every form of conflict. Poor Polly came away from marital spats feeling trampled, squashed, and left to lick her wounds—while Kurt went on to the next activity unscathed.

Later that evening, Polly called Ann again. "I feel so much better. The praise music pulled me up out of the pit. The kids started singing along, too, and even picked their toys up without being asked."

Ann could hear the smile in Polly's voice. "That's great. I was praying."

"Kurt came home and showered while I got the kids ready for bed and tucked them in. Then the two of us had a nice quiet dinner together. It really worked out nicely. Thanks for the advice."

Several mornings later, Ann stopped unexpectedly at Polly's home to drop off a book. One of Polly's young children opened the door and told Ann, "Mommy's been crying." Following him to the kitchen, Ann found Polly frantically trying to wipe away the evidence of her tears. Her four-year-old explained in a serious, grown-up voice, "Sometimes Dad's a little hard on her." Then he walked solemnly back to the television to resume normal programming.

Ann drew Polly into her arms and held her as they prayed.

Pulling apart, Polly reached for another tissue, and Ann laid the book on the kitchen table.

"Our families are just so different. He blows up and gets over it and everything's fine—with him. My family always started working on a problem—together—before it got really big." She took a deep, shuddering breath. "He's fine after an argument—like he's gotten it out of his system. But I just die a little bit inside. And it hurts for a long time." She sniffed and shrugged her shoulders. "He says I'm just too sensitive." Ann patted Polly's shoulder and nodded to say she was listening.

WENDY AND TED'S STORY

Ted and Wendy were about as unlikely a pair as you could imagine. Wendy—tall, thin, and blonde—wore clothes like a fashion model. Ted, on the other hand, was ten years older and two inches shorter than Wendy, felt most comfortable in his holey jeans, and usually needed a haircut. The differences went far more than skin-deep. He worked at a local bookstore and played in a band on the weekends. The paycheck for her secretarial skills came from a prominent local lawyer. Furthermore, Ted's first wife had left him for another man several years before.

Many friends counseled Ted and Wendy not to try marriage for all the reasons one might expect. But they did. Five months after the wedding, they were meeting with a counselor.

Wendy sat in Darlene's kitchen one afternoon and poured out her heart. "If he loved me, he wouldn't leave all the housework for me to do when I get home. He gets home at least an hour before I do, sometimes more. Couldn't he at least put the dirty dishes in the dishwasher and run it—or empty it if it's clean? Couldn't he run the vacuum cleaner if the rug looks dirty? Couldn't he throw in a load of laundry? He lived on his own for the past couple of years. He's got to know how!" She threw her hands up in disgust.

"Have you talked to him about it?" Darlene asked.

"Of course I've told him. I've asked him how he can say he loves me if he's not willing to show me." Wendy's eyes flashed. "He told me he loved me and he'd prove it. He took me down to our basement and showed me the treadmill he'd picked up that day. A treadmill!" She could almost feel steam coming out of her ears. "Not a rose or a romantic card. Oh, no! A treadmill!"

"You don't like the treadmill?"

"We talked about getting one the other day. I wanted to go along and pick it out." Wendy sighed and shook her head. "I keep thinking that if he exercises a little more he'll get in the mood for sex. I thought guys were supposed to want it more than us girls." She frowned and looked at Darlene for confirmation.

"You're right that guys are generally the aggressors in this part of marriage." Darlene looked down and paused before speaking again. "But isn't this area of marriage a little tough for a guy who's been rejected once?"

Wendy winced. "Yeah, I guess. But I'm a new bride. I want to enjoy this part of our relationship, too. It's not like I'm ugly. There's tons of guys who would want me. Why can't he just get over his hang-ups and loosen up?"

YOUR MARRIAGE STORY

We all know someone whose marriage just didn't work out. Sadly, separation and divorce infiltrate everyone's personal circle of friends and family. And even couples who look happily married often admit that inside they feel "unhappy, unfulfilled, or unsatisfied." American marriages are experiencing bankruptcy of the heart.

Painful obstacles mar every marriage, every life. We can become tired, road weary from the difficult journey, pushed to the edge of the pit of despair. The women in these stories were discouraged and desperate for some help and hope, and I'm sure you identified with them. You may be dealing with issues that haven't been mentioned yet, but are also very painful.

Be encouraged. The verses, truths, and material you are about to read have been presented to numerous women in literally hundreds of situations. Students have included engaged women, newlyweds, "oldyweds," and even a dear saint married for forty-nine years. These women cover the gamut of rich and poor, working professionals and stay-at-home moms, the hurting and those who just wanted to make a good thing better.

Even though your circumstances are unique, the upcoming truths from God's Word and His heart will address your needs. Is there hope that your situation can be turned into a thing of beauty? Absolutely!

You're all signed up for our adventure. Come, travel with me— through hope and on to joy. (If you skipped the introduction, this is a good time to go back and catch up on how to get the most out of the rest of this book.)

> *Dear God,*
> *I'm a bit nervous starting out on this journey. Please remind me*
> *often of Your love and leading. Help me to trust and obey.*

PART TWO

Looking
Inside

Dear Creator God,

You alone know my inmost being. You

planned my days before my conception.

I choose to trust You.

Please show me Your perspective

on my life and marriage

as I take a closer look.

3

Examine Your Expectations

$\mathcal{A}$ few years ago, I lost a tiny screw that held one of the earpieces onto my favorite pair of sunglasses. After I'd obtained an eyeglass-repair kit and tried every one of the replacement screws to no avail, I gave up, stuck the parts into a drawer, and went on with life.

About six months later, I stopped at the Saturn dealership to retrieve my car after a servicing. Sliding into the driver's seat, I looked for the mints always left on my dash after an appointment. (Is there any question why this car company makes big points with those of us who appreciate "little extras"?) Alongside the mints, I noticed something taped to the dashboard: the missing screw to my sunglasses. Can you believe the repair person didn't just throw it away with whatever other lint and debris he found?

This amazing story exemplifies Saturn's commitment to

"the concept of total customer satisfaction." Has your marriage fallen short of the expectations whirling around your head and heart as you walked up the aisle of the church toward your bridegroom? Is there any kind of guarantee? What is satisfaction, and where does it come from?

WHAT DID YOU EXPECT FROM MARRIAGE?

A few weeks ago, I met a single friend for lunch. In her mid-thirties, she would like to find and marry the perfect man. "Perfect for me," she qualified as I began to quiz her about any possibilities on the horizon. I asked if she'd ever made a list of the attributes, abilities, and attitudes she wants in her "perfect" husband, to which she answered yes. Her list went something like this: loves the Lord, is honest, kind and considerate, a good leader, a good listener, loves children and children love him . . .

I asked her if there was anything in a man she felt she could *not* live with. Recently, I had heard a Christian radio program in which the speaker recommended making a list of the things you *cannot tolerate* in a potential spouse. He suggested the list be used to avoid potential marital problems. Together, my friend and I put together an impressive list of things to avoid in a man: dishonesty, unfaithfulness, harshness, uncontrolled anger, negative attitude, not careful with money, stingy, excessive, cold, distant . . .

Carla fell in love with Phil's quiet, reserved, tall-dark-and-handsome appeal. He acted like a gentleman, courted her with flowers, and displayed a tender side she had never seen in her overbearing father. Phil's interest in Carla motivated him to actively pursue her. He attended every event, contest, and concert in which she was involved. Everyone loved Phil, and they all thought he and Carla made such a cute pair. What was not to like?

The picture changed after their wedding. Phil became a couch potato after work. Carla continually badgered him to climb the ladder of success. She didn't just want to talk to him; she wanted to discuss things with him, but he didn't have much to say. When he did not respond immediately, Carla made the decisions for the family. She just wanted to scream at him, "Say something; don't just sit there!"

In reality, Carla subconsciously expected Phil to take the lead in their marriage in the same way her father had done with her mother. She was particularly pleased to have chosen a gentle man who would relate to her with kindness. She did not anticipate, nor did she understand Phil's quiet, thoughtful, unrushed leadership style. Carla could not adjust to Phil's slow pace, and she expected things accomplished within her time frame. When Phil did not act on an issue Carla wanted settled immediately, she mistook his patience for apathy.

Ted and Wendy had similar problems with expectations. Growing up, Wendy witnessed her dad pitching in around the house, helping with the cooking and cleaning, and even folding laundry. In those first few months of marriage, Wendy could not understand why Ted did not help with household chores. They both worked full-time jobs, and Ted often returned home from work in the evening before Wendy. "Why can't he get dinner started, run a damp mop over the kitchen floor if it needs it, or at least shift the clothes from the washer to the drier and start the next load of wash?"

Wendy's dad was task-oriented by nature; Ted wasn't. Ted enjoyed relationships, which was one of the characteristics that initially drew Wendy to him. It wasn't that Ted did nothing around the house. In actuality, he tried to do the things Wendy asked him to do. But he became frustrated because she only ever seemed to notice what *wasn't* done. He finally developed an attitude that said "Why try?"

Whether we have lists of expected traits we desire in our mate, or even just a general picture of what we want, what we *think* we see in a person before and during courtship is generally not a complete picture of that person. At some point after the wedding, married life affords a much more realistic understanding of the other person. As time goes by, many deficiencies surface in both partners.

Physical problems can also cause discord and disappointment. As Rich recovered from his first surgery, I jokingly asked his dad if I could take advantage of an "extended warranty." Unfortunately, humans don't come with warranties, return policies, or money-back guarantees. In fact, life offers us an undisputed truth: We will experience difficulty.

HAS MARRIAGE MET YOUR EXPECTATIONS?

So you are not satisfied. Your marriage, your mate, maybe even you have fallen far short of your original expectations. What do you do now? Get a replacement? Ask for your initial "investment" to be returned? Or live with a lifetime of disappointments?

Considering the current American divorce rate, there is no question about whether or not most people are satisfied. A great number of unsatisfied people go the "replacement route" and remarry to find the ever elusive happiness. Unfortunately, the divorce rate is even greater for remarried couples than for first-time marriages.

And what about all the work you put into a marriage? I heard an older friend affectionately tease her husband and say, "I'd never want to start over on a new man; think of all these years it's taken me to get you just about the way I want you."

Living with unfulfilled expectations is common to all human beings. Disappointment is a fact of life. Reality check: Do you realize that God has the authority and the desire to perfectly resolve any questions, problems, or concerns in *any* area of your life?

In the same way, the Spirit helps us in our weakness. We do not know what we ought to pray for, but the Spirit himself intercedes for us with groans that words cannot express. And he who searches our hearts knows the mind of the Spirit, because the Spirit intercedes for the saints in accordance with God's will. And we know that in all things God works for the good of those who love him, who have been called according to his purpose. (Romans 8:26–28)

Do You Really Know What Is Best for Your Marriage?

Have you ever bought a counted cross-stitch or needlepoint kit from a craft or sewing store? When you get home with the design of your choice, you open the instructions and read them. They tell you to iron the fabric, thread your needle with the correct beginning color, and follow the directions. On the front of the packet is a picture of the completed design. As you stitch, the front side of the material begins to look like the picture, while the back is a riot of color and zigzagged stitches. But no one will look at the back when it is framed and mounted on the wall.

Our lives are much like the design on that fabric. Each day we put more stitches into place. However, we cannot look at the front of the package to see the completed picture. Only God knows what our life will look like when we reach the last stitch.

What are you seeing when you look at your life? A bunch of odd-colored threads, seeming to run every which way? Don't you sometimes want to ask, "Does my life make any sense?" Yet, consider God's position as the Master Designer. He's the one calling the stitches, and He knows how they will all fit together.

After a meeting where I'd given this analogy, a woman told me she had visited the Far East countries where large Oriental rugs are made. At one such place of business, she observed many people working on each large rug. Each worker depended entirely on one "caller," who directed each color and style of stitch. The caller alone knew the pattern, could see the "big picture," and would see the project to completion.

Our Creator God knows the pattern for our lives, sees the "big picture," and will see our project to completion. It is as true for us today as it was when Paul penned these words to the church members in Philippi, "He who began a good work in you will carry it on to completion until the day of Christ Jesus" (Philippians 1:6). What hope this gives the believer! God is still at work in us—and in our marriages.

This concept also reminds us that our lives are part of God's plan, not the other way around. Many times our world seems to revolve around us. We make our plans. We work on our goals. We want things to go our way. But God calls life according to His plans. How good to know that

His way is always best—both for His glory and our good. God always has our best in mind.

The woman who told me the rug story went on to add one final thought. While she watched, a child made a series of incorrect stitches. Amazed, she noticed the caller did not punish or correct the boy, but adjusted the original pattern to incorporate the mistake into the overall design. Stitchers near the child were given new directions. The work never stopped, nor did the beautiful pattern suffer.

Mistakes, weaknesses, even sin are a part of human existence. Do these problems thwart God Almighty and nullify His plan for our lives? The psalmist David wrote, "All the days ordained for me were written in your book before one of them came to be" (Psalm 139:16). Can God adjust the stitches of our lives to incorporate the lessons we learn? The troubles we face? Our disappointments? Yes, God calls these adjustments grace.

We naturally see things from our own point of view. Paul told the Corinthian believers, "Now we see but a poor reflection as in a mirror; then we shall see face to face. Now I know in part; then I shall know fully, even as I am fully known" (1 Corinthians 13:12). This makes a case for God's leadership in our lives. We are called to trust and obey Him.

Trust. Is God trustworthy? We've said that He has a perfect plan for you and the world He created. Yet sometimes the hand that undergirds us seems to be the adversary. The One on whom we should depend seems to be the originator of our suffering. *How could He let this happen? For what reason must I walk this valley?* You can know God's love and still struggle with feeling loved. You can know God's faithfulness, yet wonder where He is in the midst of pain.

What if you're not sure you trust God? Can you mend mistrust in God? Yes! You learn to trust God by watching Him prove Himself faithful in your life over time. The simplest way I know to see God, besides reading of His acts in history through Scripture, is to look for Him at work in your life. Isaiah 40:29–31 says that God helps, strengthens, and sustains those who put their hope in Him. Over the years of my life, I've watched God again and again fulfill this promise in my life—in dozens and dozens of different ways. As I look back over entries in my prayer

journal, I see God through life situations that only He could bring together. I've found out that God doesn't answer the way I expect every
time, but His solution is *always* better in the end. I've discovered that God
doesn't stick to my timetable. Occasionally problems work themselves out
before I even know to call for His direct intervention—I note these as
the *extra* praises listed in my journal. Sometimes, He answers with a no.
But always, His way is best.

See God for who He is, and experience Him for who He says He is.
"Praise the LORD, all you nations; extol him, all you peoples. For great is
his love toward us, and the faithfulness of the LORD endures forever.
Praise the LORD" (Psalm 117). Dear one, rest securely in the foundational knowledge that you can always trust God. He is faithful. Always.
He cannot be otherwise and remain God. He will not fail you, nor forsake you. Just watch and He'll prove it to you—time and time again. And
He will teach you how to extend renewed trust to your unique husband,
while actively and responsibly facing and accepting your spouse's human
frailty. "The LORD is good, a refuge in times of trouble. He cares for
those who *trust* in him" (Nahum 1:7, italics added).

This perspective subtly shifts us to the understanding that life isn't
meant for *our* plans; it's meant for *God's* plan. Thinking back on all the
things God has caused or allowed in your life, in your marriage, realize
that God does not seek to make you happy, but to make you holy. God's
purpose is for your life to glorify Him. Do you believe He can help you
become holy in the midst of unfulfilled expectations and disappointments? Do you believe He can turn you and your marriage into a thing
of beauty?

God knows the end of your story. You can rely on Him to get you
through. He's always there, and He cares. There is always hope. How can
I say that with assurance? The longer I live and the more trials I go
through, the more proof I've collected in the files of my life. You can do
the same. Ask God right now for His eyes with which to see, His ears
with which to hear, and His heart and mind to guide you in His ways.
And His perfect peace will comfort your mind and your heart. "Do not
be anxious about anything, but in everything, by prayer and petition,
with thanksgiving, present your requests to God. And the peace of God,

which transcends all understanding, will guard your hearts and your minds in Christ Jesus" (Philippians 4:6–7).

Complete satisfaction will come. On that day when you stand before the throne of God, may He say, "Well done, good and faithful servant!" (Matthew 25:21). Life will be worth all the struggles when we see Him.

Rest in Him now. Remember, God knows the pattern, and He will see it to completion. That's satisfaction!

Why do you say . . .
and complain . . .
"My way is hidden from the LORD;
my cause is disregarded by my God"?
Do you not know?
Have you not heard?
The LORD is the everlasting God,
the Creator of the ends of the earth.
He will not grow tired or weary,
and his understanding no one can fathom.
He gives strength to the weary
and increases the power of the weak.
Even youths grow tired and weary,
and young men stumble and fall;
but those who hope in the LORD
will renew their strength.
They will soar on wings like eagles;
they will run and not grow weary,
they will walk and not be faint.
(Isaiah 40:27–31)

Awesome Creator,
I find hope in You. I find my strength in You. You are my satis-
faction. I will rest in You, O faithful God.

Inventory Your Identity

*I*n college, everyone thought Polly and Kurt made the perfect couple. She radiated warmth and sincerity, yet maintained a cool, calm, and collected style of organization. Nothing rattled her good-natured disposition. Everyone liked Polly, the college homecoming queen. And if they liked Polly, they loved Kurt, football captain, honor-team chairman, and president of the senior class. Kurt knew how to take charge, stir up school spirit, and inspire people to action. His active, loud, cutting-edge style made him a mover and shaker. If Kurt was on the scene, things happened. Good things.

Polly and Kurt's engagement surprised no one. Everyone considered them a classic case of "opposites attract." Kurt's father praised him for finding a wife who could keep him organized and run an efficient household. Polly's outgoing mom thought Kurt was just the one to bring out the best in her quiet, somewhat shy daughter.

These two young people were attracted by the opposite strengths in each other, but they went home to live with the other person's opposite weaknesses. Polly found Kurt to be loud about everything, even arguments, which he always had to win. He also managed to be busy all the time; even the thought of his schedule made Polly tired. She had never before noticed his dictatorial style of leadership. Polly felt busy enough caring for their expanding family, but Kurt wanted Polly to get more involved with entertaining, church work, and even try a part-time job—"just for fun," he said. Kurt found that debating an issue or brainstorming new ideas with Polly was no fun. He felt she clammed up and wouldn't share her thoughts, but he couldn't figure out why. He just couldn't get her to take part in heated, exciting discussions. He hadn't realized she was such a dull person.

On the surface, the problem seemed to be the differences between these two people. In fact, the real issue was self. Both subconsciously thought, *I am who I am, and everyone should be just like me.* They were drawn to each other because of their differences, but ultimately each believed the other person should conform to his or her way of thinking and behaving, and learn to acknowledge his or her ideas as best. We need to learn that different doesn't mean wrong; different can be good. Oh, so good!

God makes every one of His children a distinct person, fitted for the tasks He has assigned to each one since before creation. You and I are given an *internal fingerprint* unlike any other in existence, one that comes with emotional, mental, social, and spiritual characteristics. We each possess a unique configuration of behavior or personality styles, learning skills, thought patterns, and love languages (ways to express and feel love). We are also given gifts, talents, abilities, and skills that come naturally, *plus* the ability to learn and add to our composite makeup. The psalmist David profoundly stated that we are "fearfully and wonderfully made." Read the full account of his praise to God, the Creator, and echo these words in your heart to God.

O LORD, you have searched me and you know me. You know when I sit and when I rise;

you perceive my thoughts from afar. You discern my going out and my lying down; you are familiar with all my ways. Before a word is on my tongue you know it completely, O LORD. . . . For you created my inmost being; you knit me together in my mother's womb. I praise you because I am fearfully and wonderfully made; your works are wonderful, I know that full well. My frame was not hidden from you when I was made in the secret place. When I was woven together in the depths of the earth, your eyes saw my unformed body. All the days ordained for me were written in your book before one of them came to be. (Psalm 139:1–4, 13–16)

Isn't it exciting and scary, all at the same time, to understand that God knows you even better than you know yourself? To me, this knowledge brings relief. God created me and knows me intimately, yet He still loves me! And He wants to help me be the wife He designed me to be.

In order to understand how your unique marriage can work, you must first discover your own personal *internal fingerprint* and that of your husband.

Read the remainder of this chapter to discover your unique blend of personality types, thinking styles, and love languages. After you identify yourself according to the following categories, go back and study your husband using the same criteria. Finally, you will want to compare your strengths, weaknesses, and the patterns that emerge with your husband's. Don't be alarmed—whatever you find out is neither "right" or "wrong"; it is merely a guide to help you better relate to each other. The purpose of this information and its application is to enhance your understanding and communication within marriage.

PERSONALITY TYPES

Personality is my favorite place to start, because this is where I first began to appreciate the major differences between Rich and me. He came home from a seminar just three years after we were married and asked me to take a "test" the seminar participants had each been given. When I finished the test, he scored it, and suddenly he pulled me into his arms and hugged me. When I asked what had elicited such a response, he looked sheepish and admitted that he had begun to take me for granted since our marriage. He explained that without trying to understand where I was coming from, he had been expecting me to be like him. And he told me how much he loved the person God created me to be.

When Rich came home with the personality test and showed me the breakdown of four possible types of people, I discovered a theory about who we are in relationship to God. I believe that God may have divided His perfect nature or personality into sections, giving each person only a fraction of who He is. In doing this, a need for fulfillment is created in each one of us—we are insufficient in and of ourselves. On a spiritual level, we need the Holy Spirit of God to work in us; He is our help in areas of weakness. And on a human plane, we need each other within the family of God. This final point is illustrated and supported in I Corinthians, where Paul says we are one body with many parts.

> *There are different kinds of gifts, but the same Spirit. There are different kinds of service, but the same Lord. There are different kinds of working, but the same God works all of them in all men. . . . The body is a unit, though it is made up of many parts; and though all its parts are many, they form one body. So it is with Christ. For we were all baptized by one Spirit into one body—whether Jews or Greeks, slave or free—and we were all given the one Spirit to drink. (1 Corinthians 12:4–6, 12–13)*

What does all this have to do with personality? Just as your body has many parts such as ears, eyes, mouth, hands, and feet, so the body of Christ (all people who believe in God and have accepted Jesus as their Savior) has many parts. Some Christians are the eyes of the body; they are visionaries for the church. The ears of the church could be the counselors who listen to those who are hurting and need encouragement. Pastors, evangelists, and teachers might represent the mouth of the church, while helpers could be hands, and missionaries the feet of the body. Where do you fit into the body of believers? How do you fit into your own marriage?

For centuries, philosophers have divided the human personality into four parts—assigning different names to the parts but, in essence, identifying the same four parts of a whole. A person can be *sanguine, choleric, melancholy,* or *phlegmatic,* although most people are a combination of two of the personalities, one being dominant. Not one of us is created identical to another, so we only tend toward one or two of these four designations.[1]

A woman with a *sanguine* personality can be the life-of-the-party. She is bubbly, talkative, and often very popular in a group setting. She loves to please people and have fun. Optimistic and spontaneous, she is always coming up with creative new ideas, but her follow-though is less than the best and she must write down anything she needs to remember.

One of a sanguine's deepest desires throughout life is to have fun! Her need for attention, affection, approval, and acceptance motivate her actions and speech. In fact, a sanguine feels let down when life is not fun and no one seems to appreciate her. This woman will color your world. She possesses creativity, optimism, and the "light touch." She has a knack for cheering up people and entertaining with style. Of course, she could work on improving her organization skills, not talking so much, and making promptness a priority. All in all, this excitable individual has great potential to be an inspirational encourager.

A *choleric* woman is a realistic, result-oriented leader. Not afraid to forge ahead, she is decisive, motivated by challenge, and fiercely independent; a powerful force to be reckoned with. She fearlessly asks "why?" and challenges the status quo—she even relishes a good argument. She feels insecure only when a situation is out of her control. The choleric's key word is control.

A choleric needs appreciation for her accomplishments and credit for her ability. That ability includes taking charge of anything instantly and making quick, correct judgments. Losing control of anything (for example: losing a job, not being promoted, becoming seriously ill, having a re-bellious child or unsupportive mate) is cause for major frustration. The fact that a choleric wife is a natural leader can prove to be a challenge in a marriage where God asks her to respect her husband. The "opposites at-tract" tendency further complicates the picture, as she is probably mar-ried to a low-key, relaxed phlegmatic. She can naturally feel he never accomplishes enough or gets excited over her projects. However, when they learn to appreciate each other's God-given strengths, a wonderfully fulfilling marriage can result.

Melancholies are serious, careful, task-oriented people. To this type of woman, it's not good enough to get a job done, she must to do it correctly. She likes to organize everything and maintain order in her world, even if it doesn't always appear that way on the surface. She dots every *i* and crosses every *t*. She loves structure, patterns, and formulas—in music, art, and life in general.

The melancholy tries to do everything the *right* way. Her needs include a sense of stability, space, silence, sensitivity, and support. She gets depressed when life is out of order, standards aren't met, and no one seems to care. She deplores compromising her standards, making mistakes, and having her feelings misunderstood. When stressed out, she might withdraw, get lost in a book, or find a safe friend with whom she can recount her problems. This hard worker possesses a great attention to detail, a love for analysis, excellent follow-through, high standards of performance, and strong compassion for the hurting. Her serious, sensitive nature flows from deep inner strengths.

A *phlegmatic* person is an easygoing, loyal, steady friend. She shies away from the limelight, but she can be found in the background ready to lend a hand. She loves people and is a dedicated, one-on-one friend who really listens to what you are telling her. And she's rarely in a rush.

This personality type is often hardest to identify, because a phlegmatic craves peace and will do almost anything to avoid a confrontation. This means that, although generally low-key, she has the ability to temporarily exhibit other personalities' strengths in order to help keep the peace. While this phenomenon makes it difficult to identify her personality (because she might seem like one or more of the others), we might describe this person as "all-purpose."

In addition to peace, the phlegmatic woman desires a sense of respect and a feeling of worth, understanding, and emotional support from friends, family, and colleagues. She possesses an even disposition, dry sense of humor, and pleasing spirit, but often struggles from a lack of

decisiveness, enthusiasm, and energy. Improvement comes with goal setting, a faster pace, and facing her own problems head-on. She is especially
valued for her abilities to be calm, cool, and collected, mediate between
contentious people, and objectively solve other people's problems. A variety of studies indicate that as much as 70 percent of the world's popula-
tion could be phlegmatic.

At this point, let me insert a very important remark about personalities. No one type of personality is better or more valuable than another.
Although you might be tempted to think "the grass is greener on the
other side" (or, on the flip side, wish everyone were more like you), make
sure you appreciate the fact that God deliberately created each one of us
with His choice of personality for the work He's calling us to do.

I have a very sanguine personality; I'm playful, talkative, and often
the life of the party. It only makes sense that God has allowed me to be a
Bible teacher, speaker, and singer, ministering in an up-front capacity to
His daughters. And I've learned to compensate for weaknesses like for-
getfulness by writing *everything* down on paper. Sure, I still fail and miss an
appointment or errand here or there, but I'm a much more effective person than I once was. That is because I've admitted to myself that I'm forgetful, and I've determined what I can do to counteract that nasty trait.
By the way, being forgetful does have one great side effect—I hardly ever
carry a grudge!

Rich and I are very different, and yet in some ways similar. Rich is
the planner, and I'm spontaneous. He organizes meticulously, whereas
I'm more a visual organizer (get it out of sight so the house looks nice
for company—and pray they don't look in the drawers or closets). He is
the cool, calculated thinker. I'm the nurturing, emotional, intuitive mem-
ber of the family. He thinks internally, and I think aloud. Yet we enjoy
many of the same interests, and we are both strong leaders (however, we
exercise different leadership styles).

Can you figure out your own personal blend of temperaments? Can
you identify your husband from the descriptions above? This knowledge
brings with it the opportunity to accept your strengths and weaknesses as
God-given and begin to adjust to the realization that you don't have to be

all things to all people. You can begin to capitalize on your areas of strength and learn to compensate for your weaknesses.

Florence Littauer, author of many excellent personality resources, reminds us: "It is amazing how other people improve when we understand their personalities and don't try to make them become like us. What a blessing it is when we can learn to accept the slightly irregular *just as they are.*"[2]

THOUGHT PATTERNS

Thought patterns are another area in which people can be as different as night and day. Early in our marriage, Rich and I had some disastrous "discussions." One of us would bring up the problem, and then Rich would sit without saying a word, while I thought through possible solutions aloud. Remember, earlier I mentioned that he thinks internally, while I need to verbalize my thoughts. I was under the impression that Rich wasn't interested in cooperatively discussing the problem, while he wished I would shut up and let him think! Our solution has worked well for years. When one of us brings up a topic for discussion, I leave the room and work on a chore or project for a short time while Rich thinks, and then I rejoin him and verbally think my way to the same conclusion he reached before I reentered the room. If we disagree, we talk out the details.

There are three modes in which people process mental information. In each area, I believe most people are not at one extreme or the other, but in fact on a continuum between the two ends.

In the area of *perceiving information,* you can be an *abstract* thinker or see things in a more *concrete* way. An abstract thinker is imaginative, intuitive, and sees what *could be,* not necessarily only what *is.* This person might enjoy looking at an abstract painting or reading an allegory. The other person thinks in concrete terms, the here and now. Using the five senses, relishing details, and seeing what is, this person enjoys looking at photographs and reading biographies of real people. If these two people were to go outside on a sunny day, the concrete thinker would see puffy, white clouds, but the abstract thinker would see shapes.

In the area of *ordering information* in one's mind, some people need more structure than others. In this arena, we have the *sequential* person and the *random* thinker. The sequential person likes lists, steps, and plans. The motto of the random thinker is "just get it done." The random thinker is spontaneous and appears disorganized, although he most often knows just where everything is.

In the area of *applying information,* one is generally *analytical* or *global.* To be analytical means you are objective, logical, and detail-oriented. Global thinkers, on the other hand, see the big picture, and they are flexible and relationship-oriented. A typical example of the global thinker is my daughter, Becky. In her early years, Rich and I marveled at Becky's ability to grasp concepts. She would often enter an adult conversation with a pertinent, well-timed comment.

When Becky got to kindergarten, she got hung up on reading. She could spell "cat," but she couldn't read it in a book. "I don't know that word," she would tell me. When she entered first grade, she told the teacher, "I can't read." Somewhere along the line, I realized that she was not breaking words into letters and letter sounds; she was looking at each word as a whole (big picture). When I taught her a good number of sight words to give her confidence, and then showed her the patterns in words she now knew, she caught on. Just a year later, we couldn't get her to put down chapter books!

As a highly global thinker, she processes information from a "big picture" viewpoint and needs help to break the picture down into bite-size details to work through. On the other hand, the analytical thinker needs help seeing how all the little pieces fit together in the big picture. Are you an abstract or a concrete thinker? Do you organize your thoughts sequentially, or are you a spontaneously random person? Do you enjoy details with the analytical person, or do you see the "big picture" as does the global thinker? Where are you in light of each area, and toward which end does your husband naturally gravitate?

LOVE LANGUAGES

Love languages are the last area of individualism we will look at in this chapter. The five love languages, as reported by Gary Chapman in several books he has written, are the ways we express and receive love from others. He suggests that you ask yourself what makes you feel most loved: *words* of love, appreciation, and affection; thoughtful and loving *gifts* (not necessarily costly—as simple as a flower from the garden that says the person is thinking of you); *acts of kindness* and service; affectionate and loving *touch*; or *quality time* spent with the one you love.

It is interesting to note that we often approach others or relate to them from our own perspective—our own individual tendencies and preferences. For example, I feel incredibly loved when someone puts a hand on my shoulder or holds me close. Not Rich. His love language is acts of service. Keeping clean, folded, and ironed clothes in his drawer and homemade ice tea in the fridge is the best way I can tell him I truly love him. For years I stroked his arms, ran my fingers across his shoulders, and massaged his feet. For years, I felt like a slave as he made it very obvious that I should launder the clothes twice weekly and keep fresh tea in the fridge at all times. *What a tyrant*, I thought more than once. Until I studied the love languages. Yes, it is a challenge to learn a new language, and it takes more effort on my part to express my love the way he understands. But doing the laundry and making tea have become rich expressions of my love for my husband.

Gary Chapman says, "Being sincere is not enough. We must be willing to learn our spouse's primary love language if we are to be effective communicators of love."[3]

A beautiful benefit of learning to speak your husband's language (even if he never learns yours) is the ability to identify his love shown toward you through his language. Often we miss the love shown to us because we do not recognize it for what it is. Remember, we all subconsciously communicate first and foremost through our own personal languages. It takes effort on our part to understand others and communicate effectively. The rewards of this effort are priceless.

Polly wanted Kurt to be more gentle and understanding, to treat her like she treated him. Kurt desired a wife who responded with spunk and fire, someone who could go head-to-head with him in a good discussion. They fell in love with each other's opposite strengths, but they went home to live with each other's opposite weaknesses. Have you and your husband done the same?

The Golden Rule says "do unto others as you would have them do unto you," but it doesn't say "expect others to act in the same way you do." We are not created the same—we are delightfully different. Look at God's creation, at the vast array of different plant life, animals, sea creatures, and more. Different is wonderful. And our way is not always the best way . . . which is a good truth to remember in marriage.

Identify who God has created you to be. Accept yourself—strengths and weaknesses. Learn to capitalize on the strengths and compensate for the weaknesses. And begin to enjoy being yourself! Then do the same for your husband. Study, identify, and understand him. Accept him in total. Complement (which means "complete") him—shore up his areas of weakness when appropriate.

Decipher the differences between the two of you—and appreciate them. Yes, differences can sometimes be irritating, difficult, and troublesome. But God created you and your mate as you are for your own good and for His glory. Appreciate how you fit together like pieces of a puzzle —and glorify God!

Studying and understanding a person is well worth the cost, but it will require time, effort, and tools. You are now equipped with some basic tools, but you must make a serious commitment of time and effort to use them wisely. Asking the Creator God to instruct and reveal the truth about yourself and your husband is also a step in the right direction.

COMPARISON CHART OF DIFFERENCES

Use this chart to compare who you are with who your husband is. After reading the chapter, fill in this chart for you and for him. Because a person is not all of one attribute and none of another, you cannot necessarily check one box in each section. I suggest you put a percentage figure in each box. (For example, in the "Me" column I might fill in 20% across from Choleric, 80% beside Sanguine, and nothing for Phlegmatic and Melancholy; 10% next to Abstract and 90% beside Concrete; and so on.)

Category	Me	My Husband
Personality Types		
Choleric		
Sanguine		
Phlegmatic		
Melancholy		
Thought Patterns		
Abstract		
Concrete		
Sequential		
Random		
Analytical		
Global		
Love Languages		
Words of Affirmation		
Gifts		
Acts of Service		
Touch		
Quality Time		

Given this information, what specific ways can you adjust your life to get along better with your husband and relate to him on his terms?

> *God of the Universe,*
> *Who am I that You would care about me? But You do! You*
> *planned my unique, one-of-a-kind existence to the most minute*
> *detail. I trust You, O God, to finish the work You've begun in me.*

Delight in Differences

About ten years into Polly and Kurt's marriage, we find them in a large home with four children, a dog, three cats, and a tank of tropical fish. Kurt continues to work with his father and brother in a diverse company with many enterprises going at the same time. Kurt thrives on the variety, high-stress, and fast-paced administrative responsibilities of the company. Polly remains quiet, almost withdrawn. She smiles shyly when we see her at church or around town, but there is a sadness in her eyes. Conversation centers around the kids, and we notice it is increasingly difficult to have a deep conversation with her. Everything looks good on the outside, but we don't see Kurt's frustrated bursts of temper or Polly's silent tears behind the front door of their beautiful home.

Polly struggles to do everything Kurt wants her to do at

home. He says he doesn't care what she does as long as she's happy, but she knows his idea of happiness is keeping busy, doing fun and exciting things, accomplishing tasks, being recognized and honored by the public—all things she shies away from. Polly would do anything for Kurt. She has always adored him, but she can't seem to please him, no matter how hard she tries. The house is spotless; the kids well-behaved and respectful; every dinner party an extravagant success. But Polly is tired and disappointed with herself for not being able to satisfy Kurt. She's at a loss for words to explain how she feels. Besides, Kurt always does all the talking.

Kurt feels as if he's going to blow up. Why doesn't Polly communicate with him? Something's wrong, he can feel it. It frustrates him that she won't open up. What makes her so sad? He has given her everything—a gorgeous home, beautiful kids, time and money to play with—what more could anyone want? He certainly wouldn't mind having a month or two to do anything he pleased—and her whole life's like that. Is she still sore at him for blowing up at breakfast the other day? OK, he admits his temper runs on a short fuse. But she knew about that when she agreed to marry him. And she knows he doesn't really mean what he says when he gets keyed up. He is always ready to kiss and make up—after all, that's the best part about fighting! He just wishes he wasn't kissing an ice maiden.

Do you remember when you thought your husband was perfect, and he thought the same about you? What has happened since then? Did your opinions of each other move from the optimistic rose-colored-glasses view through realism to perhaps a frustrated picture of people filled with faults? With God's help, you can rediscover each other's strengths, relax in grace, and regain the thrill of being gloriously different!

REDISCOVER EACH OTHER'S STRENGTHS

God created Polly and Kurt with two very different sets of *internal fingerprints.* For ten years, Polly interpreted Kurt's communication to mean she was a failure—lazy, selfish, cold. She tried to conform to his standards and reach his expectations for her, but she could not succeed. Polly felt Kurt didn't love her anymore or accept her as she was.

Polly needed to be reminded of the reasons Kurt initially fell in love with her and asked her to be his wife. During a peaceful moment at home, she finally worked up the nerve to ask him. He happily reminisced, creating a long list of glowing accolades that began to warm Polly's frozen heart. The same exercise served as a wake-up call for Kurt, who realized he had been trying to stuff Polly into his own mold.

To rediscover your husband's strengths, you must be willing to see the positive things in his past and the good things about the present man. Sound simple? Sometimes it is next to impossible to see good when our perspective gets truly mixed-up and turned around. Yet, God commands us to see "whatever is true, whatever is noble, whatever is right, whatever is pure, whatever is lovely, whatever is admirable," and "if anything is excellent or praiseworthy—think about such things" (Philippians 4:8).

What is good about your husband? What is good about you? Ask your husband what he loved about you when you were first dating. Go back to the last chapter and look down the list of positive traits that come from your personality type. Ask God to reveal the beautiful detailing He used to enhance your life. And enjoy being married to your unique husband and being you!

RELAX IN GRACE

Polly's life was filled with anxiety, insecurity, and guilt—hardly what God wants for His children. Were Polly's feelings Kurt's fault? Yes and no. Yes, Kurt needed to be more understanding. But Polly overreacted to Kurt's personality quirks. Their intense differences became magnified until they could only see the faults in each other. Because Kurt was the aggressor and Polly was more passive, both of them tended to see Kurt as right and Polly as wrong.

I experienced the same problem during an unpleasant time period in my own marriage. Rich, being the stronger of the two of us, was simply louder and more forceful about his needs and desires. I wanted to make him happy, because if he was pleased with me, I figured I'd benefit by his praise and appreciation. What I didn't count on was how difficult it was to please him. No matter what I did, he could find something I didn't do.

Soon I allowed my self-esteem to plummet, while my guilt and anxiety level soared.

When I remembered that God says, "Do not be anxious about anything, but in everything, by prayer and petition, with thanksgiving, present your requests to God" (Philippians 4:6), I promptly felt failure on a spiritual level as well. I couldn't pray. What did I have to be thankful about? And why should God listen to my requests if I wasn't pleasing Him?

I had to go back to Ephesians 2 again. What was that word—*grace?* "For it is by grace you have been saved, through faith—and this is not from yourselves, it is the gift of God—not by works, so that no one can boast. For we are God's workmanship, created in Christ Jesus to do good works, which God prepared in advance for us to do" (Ephesians 2:8–10). I'm never going to be good enough for God on my own. But by His grace and because of Jesus' saving blood, I'm forgiven. In addition, "if anyone is in Christ, he is a new creation; the old has gone, the new has come!" (2 Corinthians 5:17).

How can we lose the stress, anxiety, insecurity, and guilt in our lives? The Cross reminds us of grace and grants us freedom to rejoice in whom God created us to be. What happens if we keep making mistakes? There is no if—life includes mistakes. But mistakes afford us the opportunity to experience God's grace, apologize sincerely, learn valuable lessons, suffer through the consequences, and go on with life. Put your trust in the God of grace.

But what happens when our husbands' grace is not as freely extended as God's? Many spouses hold grudges or razz their mate over mistakes, sins, or weaknesses long after the other person has apologized and tried to amend the situation. In this case, the injured party is expecting more than God does. Ask God, in a similar situation, for His eyes to see if the real problem is yours or your husband's.

Your job in life is to be holy, which means to be Christlike. God commands us to "make every effort to live in peace with all men and to be holy; without holiness no one will see the Lord" (Hebrews 12:14). Holiness isn't something you do, but the way you are. If Christ forgave your sins, you can live in grace and peace. Holiness is part of your being, and living in peace is something you do because you are holy.

The next verse in Hebrews 12 follows with this thought: "See to it that no one misses the grace of God and that no bitter root grows up to cause trouble and defile many." Without grace in a life, the result is unrest, bitterness, and broken relationships. The beauty of God's plan includes the opportunity for us to experience grace and demonstrate it toward others, even when they don't respond in kind. In our obedience, we are filled with peace and rest that only God's grace affords.

REGAIN THE THRILL OF BEING GLORIOUSLY DIFFERENT

When Polly and Kurt began to acknowledge what they truly loved about each other, they realized that their differences could work *for* their marriage, instead of against it. They actually put their differences to work. As Kurt told Polly how much he appreciated the wonderfully peaceful environment she created for him within their home, they both became aware of how much he needed a place away from the chaos of business, where he could recharge and renew his spirit. Polly's self-esteem began to climb, and she felt more secure about sharing ideas and thoughts with Kurt—which meant he regained a conversational partner.

Kurt began to praise her on a more regular basis for the little things she did for him, and her sparkle returned. The more they explored the differences between them, the better their relationship functioned. They both felt good about themselves and about each other. Compliments became more spontaneous, and they became friends—best friends—once again. Finally the day came when Polly actually voiced her true desire to be in the background, stay at home with the children, and do behind-the-scenes types of projects. She explained to Kurt how much she loved to see him get praise and recognition, but she told him she didn't want that for herself. She even told him she would like to be more involved with him in his businesses doing background-type things. When she suggested a list of things she could do to help him, he realized what a treasure he'd overlooked for the last ten years, wanting Polly to be something she could never be instead of appreciating what she had to offer.

Look at your two hands. Spread the fingers of each hand open. Now, slide the fingers of both hands together, so that the fingers on one hand fill up the space between the fingers of your other hand. This is a great picture of marriage. The tips of your fingers are your strengths, and the valleys between fingers are weaknesses. Look how the "strengths" of one hand fill in the "weaknesses" of the other hand. So should your husband's strengths complement your weaknesses, and your strengths compensate for his areas of weakness.

Man and woman are created physically different. He is taller, harder, stronger, and usually warmer. She is generally smaller, softer, and weaker —often possessing cold feet. Skin texture, hair, size, and shape are uniquely different, creating the possibility for a phenomenon called "attraction." Go ahead, delight in your God-designed differences!

Don't minimize the beauty of the other person or the internal fingerprint that makes each of you a "one-of-a-kind." Stick to the positives— enjoy the good stuff. Compliment your mate, as you complement him. And regain the thrill of being the person God created you to be in your unique marriage.

Although God created us each to be unique individuals, one of His purposes for believers is unity—unity through diversity. God's Word has this to say about our role in marriage or any other relationship:

> *If you have any encouragement from being united with Christ, if any comfort from his love, if any fellowship with the Spirit, if any tenderness and compassion, then make my joy complete by being like-minded, having the same love, being one in spirit and purpose. Do nothing out of selfish ambition or vain conceit, but in humility consider others better than yourselves. Each of you should look not only to your own interests, but also to the interests of others.* (Philippians 2:1–4)

We find encouragement, love, fellowship, tenderness, and compassion in our relationship with God. Therefore, we have a responsibility to mirror these qualities for others. Unity requires time and effort to put yourself in the "other person's shoes." God challenges us to understand the other person. He asks us to put aside our own needs and desires and give the other person due consideration. This does not mean we are to downgrade ourselves. It does mean we are to stop thinking entirely from our own point of view and consider where the other person is coming from.

Perhaps these closing points will help you further understand the responsibility that comes with these new relationship tools.

- We tend to relate to people from our personal perspective. Pray to be less selfish and more aware of others.
- Realize that knowing another person takes time and commitment. Make time. Make the commitment.
- Learn to capitalize on your strengths and compensate (and trust God) for weak areas.
- Realize that God brought you and your husband together to "complement" (complete) and "compliment" (bring praise to) each other. Look at his weaknesses as areas where you can encourage and come alongside him.
- Don't use weaknesses as excuses. Learn to overcome and compensate.
- Remember that *no one* on earth is *perfect* . . . but we can be "complete, not lacking anything" (James 1:4).
- Don't label, limit, or box a person into a set image of who you think he is. Be flexible, open, and willing to accept nuances and shades of difference that can color your overall picture of the person with even greater beauty and richness.
- Enjoy who you are, and enjoy your unique husband!

O Perfect God,
Please give me eyes to see the strengths You placed in my husband.
Help me appreciate his potential and cheer him on in ways that
will truly encourage him to be what You've called him to be.

PART THREE

Getting Real

Dear Father God,
Some days I really don't want
to grow up—especially if it means
abandoning my fairy-tale dreams and
teddy bear. And I don't like life
when it hurts. All-Knowing One,
why can't everything be fair
and turn out happily ever after?

Forget the Fairy Tales

*O*nce upon a time (actually the date was July 29, 1981), a common girl married a real prince—and the world watched. *People* magazine reported,

> *This joyous ceremony boosted the national spirit and captivated some 750 million people around the world who watched on TV. Among the 2,500 guests were Princess Grace of Monaco, First Lady Nancy Reagan and Prime Minister Margaret Thatcher. The palace staff worked to acknowledge some 47,000 letters of congratulations and 10,000 presents, and $400 million worth of wedding souvenirs were sold worldwide.[1]*

Did you know that five copies of the voluminous wedding gown, each crafted from forty yards of ivory English silk, existed as backups for the actual wedding ceremony? Diana, Princess of Wales, epitomized the Cinderella dream.

However, the story of Prince Charles and his lovely princess did not end "happily ever after." Within six years following the ceremony, the world knew the fairy tale had ended. Sadder still was Princess Diana's untimely death on August 31, 1997.

Now, let me tell you about a different couple, happily married for fifty-three years as I write these words. Both husband and wife possess good health, a sterling list of lifelong accomplishments, and a deep and abiding love for each other. Only a tiny fraction of a percent of the world knows these two wonderful people . . . they are my parents.

Would you rather live in a fairy-tale marriage or in a marriage made in heaven? Basically, you have a choice. You can choose your perspective. As you read the thoughts about fairy-tale myths and God's truths, search yourself and your desires carefully to see where you stand on these issues.

THE MYTHS EXPOSED

MYTH I: You Must Be Beautiful to Be Loved

Even if the heroine starts out with smudges of soot on her face, she's always gorgeous after a shower and change of clothes (or a "poof" of her fairy godmother's wand). In a crowd of people, what percentage of the women are flawlessly beautiful? How many American women have grown up watching the Miss America Pageant year after year and wishing they could be the winner (or at least look good enough to make it to the contest in Atlantic City)?

Of course, Cinderella wasn't just beautiful on the outside. She could possibly be described as soft-spoken yet entertaining, meek but spirited, kind but just, laid-back yet hardworking. Know many women like that? Yet little girls (and grown-up girls) aspire to be just like her. Are you trying to be something you are not? God created you to be the perfect "you" for His purposes.

Do you feel you must attain to certain standards in order that the world (or at least your husband) will love you?

TRUTH: God loves people. He lovingly created people. He will always love people. But our sin separates us from Him and must be eradicated by His mercy. "You see, at just the right time, when we were still powerless, Christ died for the ungodly. Very rarely will anyone die for a righteous man, though for a good man someone might possibly dare to die. But God demonstrates his own love for us in this: While we were still sinners, Christ died for us" (Romans 5:6–8). God loves us, but not our sin. He loved us so much, even when we were sinners, that He provided a way to erase our sin and bring us home to Himself after this life. He loves you.

MYTH 2: You Deserve to Be Loved

Remember the old McDonald's slogan: "You deserve a break today . . . at McDonald's"? In a Loreal commercial, a gorgeous, almost naked woman is washing her hair and saying, "I use Loreal . . ." (in the next scene, she is clothed and running her hands through her magnificent thick mane of hair) ". . . because I'm worth it." Do you deserve the world's best, served on a silver platter? Of course these advertisements appeal to your desire to be beautiful and brilliant.

Other ads and commercials remind you that life is rough and you de-serve a little happiness. When you've had a terrible, horrible, no-good, awful day, you should be able to put your feet up, relax, and be pam-pered. Sorry, ladies, that day may come after Junior has grown out of his diapers, played every sport in the book, and spent all your savings on his college tuition. But the cold hard reality is life can be unfair.

TRUTH: As sinners, we deserve God's damnation. But He has given us His mercy and grace. Nothing about the real me measures up to the goodness and glory of God. My sin separated me from His presence, "for all have sinned and fall short of the glory of God" (Romans 3:23). Even my good deeds and "righteous acts are like filthy rags" (Isaiah 64:6). Because of Jesus' death on the cross to pay for my sins, I am God's adopted daughter, seen by Him as completely righteous and worthy of His unconditional love.

As children of the King of kings and Creator God of the Universe, how can we buy into the "poor me, poor soul" identity? Every aspect of our person was wondrously designed, every situation of our life purposefully planned, before we were even a twinkle in our parents' eyes. No excuse to feel sorry for ourselves is justifiable. We are deserving of God's love because of our position as adopted children.

MYTH 3: God Should Wave His Magic Wand and "Poof" You into a Better Life

Think about the concept of a fairy godmother. Wow! Wouldn't it be exciting to have someone "poof" you into the perfect outfit the next time you look in your closet and can't find a thing to wear? Seriously though, some people see God as a fairy godfather . . . someone who, in our moment of desperation, will make everything OK. Would you really want to manipulate God to get what *you* want—knowing that, if the thing was best for you and the timing was right, God would be delighted to give it to you? To be honest, I've learned by experience that my desires and ways of filling them are often wrong. However, God always gives what's best—because He knows all.

TRUTH: God sees the "big picture" and gives us only what is best for us. Doesn't this truth evoke a sublime peace within you? There is someone who knows you better than you know yourself, loves you more than you can fathom, and knows everything that will ever happen to you. This loving Father will never allow anything to touch you that does not first pass through His hand, which holds you safe and sound. And He will never let you go.

Yes, God has the power to do anything we ask Him to do. The beauty in this truth is in allowing Him to do for us what He knows is best *in the long run,* because He perfectly works everything out for His glory and our good. He gives out of wisdom, compassion, and generosity. Jesus said, "I do not give to you as the world gives" (John 14:27). The world gives to get back in return, while God gives knowing we have nothing of value to offer Him. The world gives to ease its conscience, to "look good" or feel good. God gives sacrificially of Himself. The world gives and then asks us to return the gift, but God only gives what is best and never takes it away unless it is needful.

The psalmist said to God, "Better is one day in your courts than a thousand elsewhere; I would rather be a doorkeeper in the house of my God than dwell in the tents of the wicked. For the LORD God is a sun and shield; the LORD bestows favor and honor; no good thing does he withhold from those whose walk is blameless" (Psalm 84:10–11). How about you? God never withholds the best from His children, although the best may not always seem so at the moment.

MYTH 4: There Is a Perfect Man Out There Somewhere

Prince Charming is the perfect hero. He's tough and tender. He kills dragons and still finds time to bring home flowers and candy . . . and then possesses enough energy to stay up all evening and whisper sweet nothings in the princess's ear. This guy has money to burn, looks great, acts romantic—who wouldn't want him? What husband can live up to this?

TRUTH: God can help you and your husband become "perfect" for each other, if you allow Him to work in you. As we looked at our internal fingerprints, we saw how the strengths of one personality fit together with the weaknesses of another, and vice versa. God can help you and your husband complement each other. It takes time and effort to work together—but God designed you with this potential, as well as a need for Him to take up the slack where you are lacking.

God never promised that you, your partner, or your marriage would be perfect. But He does promise joy in the working out of your faith, because "the testing of your faith develops perseverance. Perseverance must finish its work so that you may be mature and complete, not lacking anything" (James 1:3–4). "Mature and complete, not lacking anything" sounds pretty "perfect" to me.

MYTH 5: Once Married, We'll Live *Happily Ever After*

Have you ever noticed that fairy tales almost always end with a wedding? We get the idea that this matrimonial ceremony puts an end to all problems, and it's "clear sailing" from here. Many brides make lavish wedding plans, but forget to plan for the marriage, because they believe the myth: Once we are married, we will be happy. The goal is the wedding, instead of the marriage. If falling in love with the perfect person is the goal, what comes after the wedding? Bliss? Then why am I not happy?

TRUTH: Once married, the work of choosing to love my man has just begun!

Carry this myth just a bit further. Most people live with an ever present thought: *Life will be great when I* . . . You can complete the sentence with "get a new job," "have a baby," "buy a house," "win the lottery," and so on. But the grass isn't always greener on the other side. Many lottery winners who have won large sums of money squandered it completely within months, only to return to their former financial situation or worse.

When you say *life will be great when* . . . , you are living in the future, the unknown. You cannot know what will happen. You can only wish and dream. I'm not talking about being a visionary. I'm not talking about looking ahead, making wise goals, and planning objectives to reach them. But dreams of perfection and attaining the impossible belong in the library under "fiction."

THE TRUTH EXPLORED

God's Perspective on Your Situation

The future remains in God's realm. He knows what will come to pass. *He* is omniscient. We can rest in His loving care and provision. He completely transcends anything we are able to conceive or imagine. And He works things out, not only for our good and our growth, but in the best interest of His perfect plan for the whole world!

I really want my husband to see God clearly and fall in love with Him all over again. I want Rich to come to a "burning bush" and be overwhelmed with the reality of God. I want to experience spiritual oneness with him once again. But do these "wants" fit into God's overall plan? Would my song of hope and encouragement minister as effectively to the hearts of weary, discouraged women and wives if I were living "happily ever after"? Could it be that God is using His faithfulness in my life during Rich's dark time to touch other children of God and help them see His truths?

Can we question God's good will? Yes, we can ask why and search for His purposes. We should then praise God when He allows us a peek at what He's working on. And we must ask Him for faith to continue to believe even when we don't see anything but a deep, fathomless ocean of despair.

The God of the universe is crafting the seemingly good and bad circumstances together perfectly. Take a really good look at this God who shapes our lives. The more we study His Word, listen to His Spirit, and are attuned to His activity around us, the more impressed we will be with how much we have yet to learn about Him. He and His mercies are "new every morning" (Lamentations 3:23). We can trust His faithfulness in everything. Our present, our future . . . and our "ever after."

God's Will for Your Life

Before Jesus left this earth, He prayed an amazing prayer found in John 17. Notice in verse 20, He prays for you and me: "for those who will believe in me through [the disciples'] message." In following verses, His prayer is for unity as demonstrated in the Trinity.

> *That all of them may be one, Father, just as you are in me and I am in you. May they also be in us so that the world may believe that you have sent me. I have given them the glory that you gave me, that they may be one as we are one: I in them and you in me. May they be brought to complete unity to let the world know that you sent me and have loved them even as you have loved me. (John 17:21–23)*

God desires that we be unified, because given our external differences and internal fingerprints, it is most difficult to live for others when we want everyone to be just like us. Unity is a commodity the world completely lacks. The world breeds competition, arguing, bickering, complaining, judgmentalism, and other forms of dissension. Unity in us, accomplished by the triune God, is how the world will come to experience God.

Following God's example, we must find ourselves united with Christ. We read in John 15:5, 9–12,

> *I am the vine; you are the branches. If a man remains in me and I in him, he will bear much fruit; apart from me you can do nothing. . . . As the Father has loved me, so have I loved you. Now remain in my love. If you obey my commands, you will remain in my love, just as I have obeyed my Father's commands and remain in his love. I have told you this so that my joy may be in you and that your joy may be complete. My command is this: Love each other as I have loved you.*

What hinders marital unity? Sadly, we are not found "in Christ," but each is out for his own best interests. Can just one partner change a marriage? One person who is found in Christ will find a new and fresh perspective on grace, hope, and joy. Even though the marriage situation may remain the same, the partner who lives in Christ will benefit beyond belief by seeing this same situation from God's perfect point of view.

What is it that holds you back from trusting and yielding yourself to God? What rights and expectations are you holding on to?

> *Jesus modeled perfectly this attitude toward life. He had a legitimate right to enjoy the comforts of heaven. Yet, He did not look at it as a right He should hold on to, nor did He see leaving all that was His as a sacrifice too costly to make (Philippians 2:5–11). As a result, God highly exalted Him and brought salvation to a broken world.*
>
> *Has the world convinced you that there are certain rights that you must protect? Are you trying to save your life? Have you noticed that in so doing, you are actually losing the life God wants you to have?* [2]

God's Happy Ending for Your Story

Happily ever after is within the realm of possibility. However, for most of us, it comes after this earthly life. God promises us a Prince (the Prince of Peace from Isaiah 9:6), who will be riding a white horse (Revelation 19:11). We will live and reign with God forever and ever. Accordingly, the bottom line is this: *The party is in heaven.* What is the purpose of our earthly existence? Our job is to do the work for which God uniquely designed and equipped us. In light of eternity, this life is short. It will soon be gone. We can hang in there.

Indeed, God's Word and His Spirit encourage us to do much more than simply hang on till the end. God's gift of salvation gives the believer not only *eternal* life but *abundant* life! So much is possible: peace, joy, contentment, and love . . . even romance.

There is hope—but it is on God's terms, not according to the standards of this world. Think about it. Isn't it time to let go of the fairy tales of an imaginary world, and choose to get to know the real God who offers to us an abundant life in this world and then in heaven forever after?

> *"I know the plans I have for you," declares the LORD, "plans to prosper you and not to harm you, plans to give you hope and a future. Then you will call upon me and come and pray to me, and I will listen to you. You will seek me and find me when you seek me with all your heart." (Jeremiah 29:11–13)*

> *Dear God,*
> *I gratefully acknowledge Your gift of real hope. I accept it on Your terms, relinquishing any prior hopes or dreams based on the standards of this world. I choose to trust You.*

7

Give Up False Guilt

Meghan could hardly look at her husband when he got home from work. She really wanted to hide. For the past three days he'd been asking for clean, pressed dress shirts, a new tube of toothpaste, and a box of thank-you notes. Actually he had asked her for the thank-you notes several times in the past few weeks. She was so afraid he was going to ask her what she'd done all day long. Just what *had* taken all her time? She ran through an unimpressive list of chores, errands, and projects she'd worked on while the kids were at school. Of course the half hour on the phone to her sister and a long discussion with the next-door neighbor had eaten a good portion out of her day.

She could sense Keith's frustration with her as he passed through the kitchen on his way to the bedroom to change into more comfortable clothes before dinner. Without really thinking, Meghan lifted the cookie-jar lid and grabbed a cookie, hoping the kids weren't watching. Just after she'd swallowed the last crumb, six-year-old Allison ran into the room and wrapped her arms around Meghan—at least she tried to get her arms around Mom's ever expanding waistline. "No wonder he can't stand the sight of me," Meghan muttered to herself, as Allison turned around and waltzed out of the room. Feeling defeated and unhappy, she slipped another cookie into her mouth.

Reality fell far short of Meghan's grand expectations for herself, her husband, and their marriage, as it does for most of us. Inflated expectations cause disappointment, frustration, and/or guilt. Are you feeling guilty right now because of something you wish you had done or not done? Are you an approval seeker? Do you need a certain number of "pats on the back" each week to feel good about yourself? If you've answered yes, you are in good company. We all want to be accepted, approved, and applauded.

But we're people. We goof up. We expect too much of ourselves and fall short of the mark. And then we become discouraged. Discouragement rarely leads us to a solution to our problems; it most often hinders us from moving in the right direction. As with Meghan, many of us are weary from the load of guilt we carry. And we console ourselves with poor substitutes that often cause more guilt and despair. Guilt, guilt, and more guilt.

Do you realize that some of the "guilt" we feel is not guilt at all, but disappointment in ourselves? Satan capitalizes on these feelings and effectively uses them to defeat us. We suffer from "false guilt" when we try too hard to meet expectations, fall short, and then feel "guilty" about failing. True guilt comes from the Holy Spirit, as He convicts us for real sin—doing something against God.

Let me give you an example of true guilt in my own life. Rich had asked me to pick up a birthday card and mail it to a family friend. I waited several days, was reminded once, and then stuck it in the mail just moments before Rich asked me yet again if I'd mailed the card. "Yes," I said, not meeting his eyes, "it's in the mail." True, but it was about a hundred feet from us, sitting in the mailbox, which was not quite what he had in mind when he asked the question. My conscience (prompted by the

Holy Spirit) quickly reminded me that in actuality I was lying to Rich. I tried to argue and rationalize that what I'd said was a half-truth, but He was right—I lied. Yes, I had to tell God I knew I'd lied. Then I had to tell Rich and ask him to forgive me.

True guilt is immediately removed from our lives when we confess our sin to God. "If we confess our sins, he is faithful and just and will forgive our sins and purify us from all unrighteousness" (1 John 1:9). Please note, I said the *guilt* is removed—not necessarily the *consequences* of our actions.

"When we *confess* our sins . . ." Many people incorrectly think confession is asking for forgiveness. Confession literally means *to agree with* God that what you did was sin. Along with our confession, God desires a repentant heart and a will to turn from our sin toward Him.

"False guilt" is not really guilt at all, but disappointment based on unrealistic expectations. False guilt can be caused by three different situations. First, I can feel guilty or disappointed in myself if I don't meet my own expectations. Second, I can feel guilty because I can't reach someone else's expectations. And third, I can feel guilty because I *think* someone expects something of me that, in actuality, the person doesn't really care about. Let me explain each area of false guilt and show you how to combat it.

Are You Expecting Too Much from Yourself?

The first area of false guilt arises for me when my own personal expectations are too high. I get Becky off to school at 8:15 A.M. and then try to complete four loads of laundry, major housecleaning, the weekly grocery shopping, baking, and monthly banking before Becky comes home from school at 2:45 P.M. OK, before you laugh at me, look at the things you try to cram into your own schedule. Or how about the disappointment you feel when your dreams don't come true? All of this has to do with inflated personal expectations.

In the first type of false guilt, take stock of your situation. Appreciate the good aspects, ask what is really most important right now, and work on achieving only what really matters. In the example of trying to stuff too much into my schedule, I need to be realistic. I can list what needs to be done and prioritize the list according to what is most important, but then I must be satisfied with whatever I am able to accomplish. All I can ask of myself is to do my best.

I am learning that this area of expectation is not easily conquered. Having a balanced view of what I want to do, need to do, and am able to do is only possible by the grace of God and according to how closely I walk with the Holy Spirit. If I remain in touch with Him and allow Him to rule my life, my day, and each moment, I can live victoriously over the expectations in my life. I am praying for you, even as you, too, struggle to keep in step with God.

IS SOMEONE ELSE EXPECTING TOO MUCH FROM YOU?

The second area of false guilt comes from someone else expecting too much from you. Are you married to a demanding person? Did your husband ever call at four o'clock in the afternoon and tell you he's bringing his boss and several co-workers home for dinner at five-thirty? At our house, impromptu entertaining is the norm, but if Rich doesn't give me enough time to fix a meal, I don't feel guilty about asking him to pick up pizza on his way home. False guilt would be feeling disappointed in myself because I know Rich would have liked a home-cooked meal and I think I should have somehow been able to pull off an impossible situation.

In this second type of false guilt, when someone else is placing unrealistic expectations on you, look at the situation objectively. Don't let your hurt emotions get the best of you. A year or so ago, I had photos developed to use on a Christmas card. When I went to pick up the pictures, I felt confident about which pose was best. So I went ahead and ordered the cards without first showing them to Rich. When I got home, I was appalled to find out he didn't like any of the pictures—not even the one I'd selected . . . and ordered! He let me know in no uncertain terms that I'd really goofed up. He asked how I could possibly have thought the picture was acceptable. Instead of feeling guilty that I had not pleased him, I looked objectively at the whole situation. I liked the picture; he didn't. What could be done from here? I picked up the phone as I said to

Rich in a calm voice, "Let me call and put a hold on the order until we can decide what we want to do."

Sure, I still feel bad when Rich is upset about something I've done. But I've learned not to take his criticism personally—especially if it was a simple mistake. And generally something, often something simple, can be done to remedy the situation or at least put it back on the right track.

At a recent speakers' conference, I heard great advice on what to do when someone criticizes you: "Swallow, smile, and say 'thank you.'" The Bible tells us that "a gentle answer turns away wrath" (Proverbs 15:1). There will always be people who want you to do more than you can do, or to be more than you are. Around those people, you must swallow, smile, and say, "Thanks for your input; I'm trying" or "Thanks for telling me how you feel."

Remember, telling people you cannot do something they expect of you is fair. Don't promise something you can't carry through on. But if you do get into a situation that is over your head, admit your weakness without being defensive and work with the person to find a solution.

Do You *Think* Someone Is Expecting More Than He Really Is?

Let's say your husband's birthday is this Friday evening. Last year, you planned a big party, inviting many of his friends, and he seemed to enjoy it very much. This year you have to watch expenses, and a party is out of the question. You feel guilty all week as you make a cake and a nice meal and wrap the one present you and the kids got for him. You rationalize that if you were working, instead of being a stay-at-home mom, there would be more money for things like this. Friday night, your husband tells you he's had a wonderful day, and although he appreciated the effort on last year's party, he loves spending time with just the family on his birthday. Then he reminds you how much he appreciates you for being willing to stay at home for the kids, even though it makes expenses a little tight. You realize you wouldn't have needed to feel so bad all week long!

This third area of false guilt is sort of sneaky. I call it "phantom guilt." It shows up when we feel as if we are letting someone else down, without really knowing what the person wanted in the first place. It's a misconception on our part. Dealing with phantom guilt involves a reality check.

Growing up, I saw my father's desire for my mom to go to bed at the same time he did each night. I transferred this desire or expectation over to Rich when we got married. I felt guilty if I had to stay up late to correct students' papers. I was disappointed in myself the next morning if I had finished watching a movie and went to bed an hour after Rich retired the night before. Then I found out Rich really doesn't care whether I'm there when he goes to sleep! I had never asked him. We just needed good communication—and I needed a reality check. If you need to deal with this type of false guilt, ask yourself, "Just what does that person want from me?" Maybe you need to ask the other person. Realize that you may be the one with the inappropriate expectation. You may be the one who has to back off, regroup, or let go.

So what is the answer to false guilt and unattainable expectations?

WHAT *SHOULD* YOU EXPECT FROM YOURSELF?

We already said we must learn to be realistic. God's expectations are the only ones that truly count, and they are very simple. "What does the LORD require of you? To act justly and to love mercy and to walk humbly with your God" (Micah 6:8). Starting every day in the presence of God is very important, and walking with Him throughout the day keeps us looking at things from His perspective.

Ask yourself, "What would Jesus want me to do in my situation right now?" And then do His will. And you will find fulfillment in meeting God's expectations for you, becoming what He's created you to be, and doing what He's prepared for you to do.

I will still be disappointed when I fail or when someone fails me, but the fact remains that God loves me. There is nothing I can do that will make Him love me less. Likewise, there is nothing I can do that will ever make Him love me more than He does at this very minute. I love Him, because He first loved me (1 John 4:19).

Give Up False Guilt

Search me, O God, and know my heart. Convict me of sin, that I might confess it and receive Your forgiveness and grace. Then free me of all expectations save Yours, and teach me the truth.

8

Accept God's Approval

What is every women looking for? Stop a moment and think about this question, while I tell you my answer. I want to feel special, to matter to someone. I want my skills and abilities to be recognized and applauded. I want to do things for other people that make a difference in their lives, and I want them to notice. Bottom line: I want to feel significant. Approval, acceptance, forgiveness, grace, hope . . . it all boils down to *significance*. Humans possess a distinct desire to feel significant.

THE LIES SATAN WANTS US TO BELIEVE

In the last two chapters we talked about the myths the world tells us and the false guilt Satan dumps on us. In this chapter, we will focus on the lies Satan wants us to buy into.

These lies of Satan will attack the issue of our significance. He wants to make us think we're not doing enough for God. He suggests to us that we'll never please our husbands, so why put forth the effort to even try? And he wants us to feel guilty when we mess up. In short, our opponent wants us to think God's approval is not enough—that we still need the acceptance and love of others to feel good.

Open your eyes to these four sneaky lies Satan uses to rob us of our significance as children of the King of kings and Lord of lords.[1]

LIE 1: I Must Meet Certain Standards in Order to Feel Good About Myself.

Polly tries to do everything perfectly—but she always fails in one tiny way or another. Not that her friends and acquaintances ever notice; to everyone else her house looks picture-perfect, her children are respectful and well-behaved, and her lavish dinner parties are the talk of the town. Everyone calls her "Martha." But Polly sees all the things that went wrong, everything that wasn't exactly right. She's so hard to please, even her husband has stopped complimenting her because she can always find some way to dismiss his positive comment with a negative one of her own.

Polly feels like a failure, no matter how hard she tries to be perfect. She has bought into Lie 1. This fear of failure results in perfectionism, avoiding risks, anger, resentment, self-condemnation, anxiety, fear, pride, and even forms of depression.

The melancholy personality is most likely to struggle with the fear of failure. Even though this person's world revolves around meeting certain standards, failure is inevitable somewhere along the line. No one is perfect; to expect to be perfect is unrealistic.

Satan, sly fox that he is, whispers, "But with God, nothing is impossible. If God is at work within you, you should be able to exceed all human expectations. You are a disappointment to God." Translate that: Because you are imperfect, God does not love you. Do you see the lie?

GOD'S TRUTH counteracts this lie with "justification." "Therefore, since we have been justified through faith, we have peace with God through our Lord Jesus Christ, through whom we have gained access by faith into this grace in which we now stand. And we rejoice in the hope of the glory of God" (Romans 5:1–2). To be justified means to be made right. How can a sinner be made right with God? Through salvation, we are completely forgiven and fully pleasing to God. The fear of failure is no longer a threat—we have peace with God.

LIE 2: I Must Have the Approval of Certain Others to Feel Good About Myself.

Meghan, on the other hand, is spontaneous and fun-loving. She's so spontaneous that she often gets into projects way over her head. She makes heartfelt promises she can't follow through on; she hopes people realize "it's the thought that counts." She feels like a terribly tyrannical mom because she seems to be constantly yelling at her kids, but in reality she's not a consistent disciplinarian. She doesn't want the kids to get mad at her, so she waits until it's almost too late to correct them, and then she yells. Her husband wishes she'd be on time, follow through when she says she'll run an errand for him, and try to get the house cleaned at least every couple months. She just can't seem to please anyone—and she tries so hard.

Meghan is desperate for approval from her husband and kids. She fears rejection above all else, which is part and parcel of Lie 2. This lie produces a person who attempts to please others at any cost, is overly sensitive to criticism, and withdraws from others to avoid disapproval.

The sanguine personality lives to please people. These people really live for the strokes and admiration of those they please; pleasing people is how they "earn" those good feelings. The sanguine/choleric keeps trying harder and harder, does more and more, while the sanguine/phlegmatic just gives up. The worst nightmare for a sanguine is rejection from anyone!

GOD'S TRUTH tramples this lie with His gift of reconciliation. "If, when we were God's enemies, we were reconciled to him through the death of his Son, how much more, having been reconciled, shall we be saved through his life! Not only is this so, but we also rejoice in God through our Lord Jesus Christ, through whom we have now received reconciliation" (Romans 5:10–11). Has the full meaning of these verses affected your being? We, who were hopelessly estranged from God because of our sin, are now His children and friends because of Jesus' death on the cross in our place. We have direct contact with God Almighty from now through eternity. He will never let us go. He loves us—unconditionally.

Do you remember what was stated in the last chapter? *There is nothing I can do that will make God love me less, and there is nothing I can do that will make God love me more than He does at this very minute.* God loves me. God loves you if you are found under the blood of His Son. Although a wife should honor her husband enough to want his approval, she doesn't really *need* his approval if she's doing the right thing. We don't ignore others' opinions of us, but God's opinion is the one that counts for all time. We can find peace for anxious moments in knowing nothing will change God's love or approval of His children. God loves us—God loves *you.*

LIE 3: Those Who Fail Are Unworthy of Love and Deserve to Be Punished.

Wendy's problem is not so much with herself—her source of irritation is her husband. She feels as though she cannot honestly reward him with her love when he does nothing to earn her respect. She says he refuses to help around the house and do little things that anybody is capable of. Although he comes home before she finishes work and she's asked and asked him to start supper and do a few chores around the house, nine out of ten times he's sitting watching television when she walks in the door. She figures she picked the wrong guy and now she's paying for it.

Wendy doesn't feel right about rewarding her husband with kind words, encouragement, and love when he's not doing anything to deserve it. She wants to fix him first, and then he'll deserve her love. She buys into Lie 3. This lie produces a person who punishes others when they don't reach a certain level of expectation. It also causes people who fail (and we all do at one point or another) to expect punishment—to feel they deserve it. Blaming self or others, withdrawing from God and fellow believers, and doing everything possible to avoid punishment—these things all stem from Lie 3.

A take-charge person, the choleric makes an excellent leader or administrator. But the strengths of this personality can be overused or misused to the extent that the choleric becomes controlling. "You've got to measure up. If you said you would do it, it had better be done. If you can do this and this and this, why can't you follow through on that? Never mind, I'll get someone else to do the job." In most cases, this person punishes himself just as hard as anyone when he's the one who has made the mistake.

Satan doesn't have to give this person much encouragement at all. He simply suggests more reasons why the person should have been able to do something that didn't get done. He tells her punishment is the only fair way to treat the problem, and it will hopefully teach the person not to repeat the crime.

GOD'S TRUTH is this: God is fair and just, but through His Son He offers us mercy and grace . . . forever. Mercy is taking away the punishment we deserve because we are sinners. Grace is giving us all the blessings He has prepared for us on earth and in heaven, even though we are undeserving. And because of God's example of grace to us, we can be gracious to others when they are wrong. "Therefore, there is now no condemnation for those who are in Christ Jesus, because through Christ Jesus the law of the Spirit of life set me free from the law of sin and death" (Romans 8:1–2). I no longer fear punishment, nor do I feel the responsibility to punish others.

LIE 4: I Am What I Am. I Cannot Change. I Am Hopeless.

Angie's husband, Nick, doesn't go to church anymore. Angie found it so difficult to get up on Sunday mornings and prepare three little ones in time to get to church, she doesn't even try anymore. She feels she has dropped the ball. It was up to her, and she failed. She knows she should go to church and take the kids, but she says she can't change—she has tried. She says she's a hopeless case.

Angie is depressed, because she can't meet the expectations she or others have set for her. She has failed so many times, she wants to give up. She is experiencing the despair of Lie 4.

How easy it is for the phlegmatic to slip into believing this lie. The strength of the phlegmatic person is in relating to people (especially when mixed with the sanguine personality). However, a phlegmatic person doesn't always get a lot accomplished—or see the need to. Without much to "show" for themselves, in a world that generally measures worth by successes, the phlegmatic person can easily become discouraged.

GOD'S TRUTH is found in regeneration. "From now on we regard no one from a worldly point of view . . . if anyone is in Christ, he is a new creation; the old has gone, the new has come!" (2 Corinthians 5:16–17). Even though this truth is real in every Christian's life, we must each take advantage of the Holy Spirit working within us to keep us from evil. Our natural sin nature is ever present until the end of this life, but we can crucify it by the power of the Holy Spirit. Listen to Paul's words to the Ephesian believers: "You were taught, with regard to your former way of life, to put off your old self, which is being corrupted by its deceitful desires; to be made new in the attitude of your minds; and to put on the new self, created to be like God in true righteousness and holiness" (Ephesians 4:22–24). You have God's power within you to help you become all He wants you to be. You must choose God's truth over Satan's lies and your own sinful desires. God can give you the victory; He can change you.

THE TRUTHS GOD WANTS US TO BELIEVE

Your Significance to God

You matter to God—the One who created the universe and hung the stars in place. You *personally* matter to God, and He wants to relate to you on an intimate level.

Satan hates God. And he hates anything that resembles God or is associated with Him. Satan will do *anything* to discredit God in your mind. Don't let him.

Accept God's approval, the mercy and grace He freely offers, and His unconditional love.

The Power in Accepting God's Love

When Polly finally came to terms with God's acceptance and uncon-ditional love, she found a wonderful freedom from the pressure of trying to be perfect. She realized that God loves her regardless of what she does or doesn't do, simply because she's His child. Now, she's trying to relax her rigid standards and enjoy the good things around her, not dwell on just negatives.

Meghan had to realize that God's opinion of her is the only one that truly counts. And He loves her unconditionally because of the Cross. Since Meghan's heart has been filled with God's love and acceptance, she no longer craves it from her husband and children. She is no longer empty, but full of God's love, which in turn she pours out on others.

When the truth of God's grace hit Wendy, she became a different person. No longer did she make demands on her husband. No longer did she find fault with him and try to put him in his place, teach him lessons, and hold back her love. The grace from God in Wendy's life spilled out on all those around her. With the encouragement he's receiving, even her husband has had a change of heart. As she encourages him, instead of putting him down, things are getting done around the house—and there is more time for the two of them to enjoy each other.

God gave Angie hope. When she realized the Bible says she can be a new creation, she took God at His word. With the help and encourage-ment of a prayer partner, Angie began praying regularly for her husband to come back to church. She began working on goals to get herself and the children back to church and growing as Christians. Her husband still doesn't go with her to church, but Angie and the kids are there every Sun-day morning.

What is your story? Are you like one of these women at the beginning of the chapter—or here at the end? The difference is in choosing to be-lieve and act on God's truth. Don't let Satan fool you with his clever lies. Our God is powerful and loving. His Word of truth gives us the hope we need to be the women and wives He's called us to be. You are precious in His sight. You are truly significant.

REMEMBER: *There is nothing you can do that will make God love you less, and there is nothing you can do that will ever make God love you more than He does at this very moment, and for all eternity.*

> *Gracious Father,*
> *Thank You for the astounding gifts of justification, reconciliation, forgiveness, and regeneration. Keep my mind stayed on You and Your truth, that I might be free from the devil's deceit.*

PART FOUR

Independence and Dependence

Dear Omnipotent One,
Without You, I am blind,
weak, and vulnerable.
Without You, my best attempts are
futile, and my life is meaningless.
I am learning that You are
my everything. In Your presence
is fullness of joy.

9

*Satisfy
Your Soul*

If God would grant one wish regarding your marriage, what would you want? These are by far the most common responses I've heard:

- "I want him to love the Lord."
- "I want a godly, Christian husband who will pray with me."
- "I'd like him to initiate devotions with me and the kids."
- "If only God would help my husband see the need for us to worship together."
- "My desire is for my husband to love me as Christ loves the church."
- "I want my husband to be the leader God designed him to be."

Don't you often wonder what it would be like to live with a man who completely emulates Jesus Christ, a man who loves you as Jesus loves His bride? And don't you think you would feel more spiritually fulfilled if your husband were a more godly man? After all, we read these words to husbands from God, in Ephesians 5:25–30:

> *Husbands, love your wives, just as Christ loved the church and gave himself up for her to make her holy, cleansing her by the washing with water through the word, and to present her to himself as a radiant church, without stain or wrinkle or any other blemish, but holy and blameless. In this same way, husbands ought to love their wives as their own bodies. He who loves his wife loves himself. After all, no one ever hated his own body, but he feeds and cares for it, just as Christ does the church—for we are members of his body.*

"I wish my husband would get back to the convictions he had when we were dating." Angie sighed and stirred a spoonful of sugar into her coffee. "Before we got married, we went to church regularly. When we moved away from my hometown, we got busy and never seemed to take the time to find a new church. When the kids came along, I thought they should grow up in a good local church. Nick agreed. We tried churches and settled on one we all liked, and we all went for a while." She paused, nibbling a bite of a cinnamon bun. "Gradually Nick's excuses not to go to church became more and more frequent. Now he only goes with us around the holidays."

As Angie wiped her mouth, she looked at Pam across the table. "I'm sure one of the biggest reasons we are not getting along well is that Nick simply has no room in his life for God. If he'd get his act together with God, all our problems would straighten out."

Have you ever felt like Angie? Do you believe that the problems and irritations in your marriage would disappear if your mate would be fully committed to God?

Or maybe your husband is a godly man who loves the Lord. Maybe he reads the Bible and prays with your family. But you still have problems.

"Why can't Phil be as committed to me as he is to God? If Phil is as godly as everybody thinks he is, how come he doesn't take a leadership position in our family?" Carla shook her finger at her friend and pressed home her point. "If everyone would sit around and read their Bible all the time like he does, nothing would ever get done! I'm the one who constantly makes the decisions and takes responsibility to see that things get done and life moves ahead. The last time I asked Phil about an issue, he told me he'd pray about it. I pray, too, but sometimes we need to move out and do what God's given us the sense to do."

Why doesn't every Christian woman have the godly husband she desires? For that matter, why don't Christians have everything they need and want? Philippians 4:19 says that "God will meet all your needs according to his glorious riches in Christ Jesus." So, how come you don't have _____ (you fill in the blank)?

DEFINING *NEED*

Needs come in many shapes, colors, and textures. One size does not fit all. Furthermore, our own personal needs fluctuate as we mature. The requirements of our childhood change as we grow into adolescence, move through adulthood, and end up in the golden years. What you put on your Christmas wish list ten years ago is probably not what you dreamed about this past year.

Perhaps a few definitions will help us begin to understand this subject. Typically, *needs, desires,* and *wants* are used interchangeably. Mr. Webster defines *need* as "a necessity or the lack of something required." A *desire* is a "wish, craving, or longing." And *want* is described as "a lack, shortage, or craving." I like to think of a *need* as "something necessary for normal existence" and a *want* as "something desired, but unnecessary for an acceptable quality of life." As you can see, both words qualify as a type of longing, but one is needful and the other is not entirely necessary.

The difference between needs and wants is easily illustrated with clothing. I took my daughter to the shoe store, because she had outgrown the black shoes she wore with Sunday dresses and nice outfits. We came home with two pairs of black shoes—the ones she *needed,* and also a pair of funky black clogs she *wanted* (and agreed to pay for with her own spending money). Actually, I believe she described the clogs as "to die for." Unfortunately, even as realistic adults, we sometimes feel the same way about our own wants.

Needs, not *wants*, are where we'll focus for the remainder of this chapter. Let's break needs down into their different levels. Surface (physical) needs cover such daily requirements as food, shelter, and clothing. Deep (internal) needs include the need to be loved, the need to be needed, the need for self-worth, and the need to be accepted by others.

Angie's phlegmatic personality needs peace, while her melancholy tendencies cry for structure and order. Guessing Angie's love language is easy—she needs a predictable amount of quiet time, spent simply with family. Within her burns an insatiable desire for quality time with her husband and kids. She also longs for a godly older woman to show her how to be the kind of wife she reads about in Proverbs 31.

My internal needs, as a sanguine-choleric, are about as opposite from Angie's as night and day. I feel fulfilled and energized when I am actively producing and when I am pleasing people. Even as I sat down at the computer to write this chapter, my parents phoned and asked if I could come now to help them take down the Christmas tree and vacuum a few rooms for them. At seventy-five and seventy-seven, their time is more valuable for grandparenting than cleaning. And I enjoy helping them in as many ways as possible. I love to be busy. Productivity and the praise of others makes me feel good about myself.

Carla's deepest needs as a melancholy-choleric are order and control. Her mind gropes for the bottom line in every conversation. She, herself, is concise—why deal with extra information that is simply not pertinent to the issue at hand? She wants closure on the issue so she can move on to the next situation. Efficiency is the name of her game; it is the reason she is able to accomplish everything.

Meghan, on the other hand, just wants to have fun. Don't overlook her very real need to be happy and enjoy what she's doing. Although she appears (to people like Carla) to be an underachiever, Meghan is loved by everyone. She's got a giant heart, a ready smile, and a kind word for the underdog. Meghan's sanguine-phlegmatic nature is uncomplicated. She needs people to love and have fun alongside.

What are the longings of your heart? In the deep places of your inner person, what do you most need in this life?

PERCEIVING NEED

The women mentioned in the last few paragraphs illustrate how each person sees life from a slightly different slant. Who we are, how we are internally "wired," plays a big part in how we perceive situations in our life, people around us—even ourselves—and what we think we need.

Just yesterday, my pre-teen complained and whined and even shed tears about her school being one of the very few open, while the other school districts had closed because of a significant snowfall. Becky's *perceived need* was to stay home from school to have fun in the snow. Because she did not have a choice in the matter, her *real need* was to overcome her disappointment and make the best of a shortened day at school.

Wendy, the young bride who had such grand expectations for her marriage, perceived her needs as met only when Ted demonstrated his love by doing kind and romantic things for her. In actuality, Wendy's core need for love and significance was not met in God first, and therefore no amount of outside affection could consistently fill Wendy's "love tank."

Polly dreams about having just one or two nights a week when she can sit around the fire and play games with her husband and kids, watch a movie, or talk. Instead, every evening is brimming with activities insisted upon by her playful husband. Kurt signs the kids up for every sport in the book, wants the kids to take a variety of music lessons, and always says yes to anyone who asks them over for a meal. The schedule is full. Even on the off chance there's nothing happening, Kurt will call on his way home from work and try to interest the family in a spontaneous night out on the town. Worn-out Polly's very real need for rest and peace must first come from the internal rest and peace of God. Then she will be able to tackle the job of finding downtime for herself, while being energized to spend active time with the family. She may also need to talk to Kurt about her desire for and the benefits of a slower-paced family night every so often.

The people in the last three paragraphs experienced perspective problems. (Polly's problem was that her perspective didn't jive with her husband's.) Each saw the situation at hand through her own version of reality. You've probably heard the expressions "put yourself in his shoes" and "she's looking through rose-colored glasses." Perception is the filter through which we focus on the world around us as it affects our lives.

My father, a professional photographer, taught me as a young child the wonders of a camera. I remember being absolutely fascinated with the filters he used to cause special effects. Yes, his expensive camera's fine lens could capture every detail of the subject and render a perfect likeness. But when he added a star filter, a polarized filter, or a sun-catcher filter, the picture took on unique aspects, sometimes drastically altering the finished image.

Are you clearly perceiving yourself, your situation, and your needs? Are your perceived needs realistic? Looking through God's eyes, which core needs remain?

OUR BOTTOM-LINE NEED

Before deep and lasting fulfillment can enter your life, a bottom-line, universal need must be examined. Yes, you may clearly understand your unique internal needs, but without fulfillment in this one chief area, you will never be completely satisfied. When this most basic need is met, fulfillment is more likely. This area of need is the God-shaped vacuum within each and every human being.

Long before Rich stopped going to church, our spiritual oneness was shaky. We didn't have devotions or pray together with regularity. For years, even when he was a youth pastor, I wished he would be a stronger spiritual leader in our home. One of the reasons for our lack of spiritual oneness, I know now, was our lack of knowledge and understanding of the other person. I expected Rich to perceive God, worship God, and serve God like I did, not accounting for the fact that Rich is my polar opposite in thinking and feeling! My expectations were way off base. I recognize now that when Rich comes back to God, I need to give him the freedom to see God from his own unique perspective. I need to allow him to be the godly leader he has been designed to be.

Why is it that we women often long more desperately for our husbands to be godly leaders in the home than we long to connect with God Himself? Perhaps this is one of Satan's clever schemes to keep us just shy

of hitting the mark. Desiring your husband to be a man of God is a noble thing, yet actually becoming a woman after God's own heart is of infinitely higher worth (and more possible, since you are only responsible
for *you*). So where are we women missing the mark? How are we getting
sidetracked?

First, many women are mistaking God-given *desire* for a spiritual head
with *need*. Desiring your husband to take his rightful spiritual role in the
home is valid. It is, literally, divine to share spiritual fellowship with our
husbands, study and worship together, and experience the peace and protection of their spiritual headship, but *these things are not crucial to our individual spiritual development.* Yes, they strengthen and build up our marriages.
Yes, they are key elements in spiritual unity. But the truth remains: We
can live joyfully with a husband who offers little or no spiritual leadership, if we enjoy a thriving personal relationship with God.

We cannot live without God. We cannot live fulfilled lives without a
right relationship with Him. Easy to say, hard to do: Let go of your desire for a human spiritual leader and trust God to be your ultimate spiritual head. God is all you truly need, and He will provide as He sees fit.

Second, many women feel they have a deeper personal relationship
with God than their husbands possess. One explanation for this reality is
this: Stereotypically, women tend to be more relationship-oriented, while
men are often more driven by tasks. (The melancholy-choleric woman
also struggles with being task-oriented, as opposed to relationship-
oriented.) Christianity is a relationship. Originated in Christ's "task" on
the cross, our relationship with God overflows and produces the fruit of
a godly life. Sometimes it takes a man a long time to develop relationship
skills that come naturally to his wife. This can be true in the spiritual
realm as well. Your man is a person who is responsible for his own relationship with God. You are not ultimately responsible for your husband's
spiritual state. Although you can pray for him and influence him by actions, reactions, and attitudes, you cannot change him. Accept him as he
is. Allow him to relate to God on his own terms. (God can handle him.)

Third, many women have preconceived ideas of what they want spiritual headship to be. Because God created men different from one another, each one will govern, lead, and guide in a unique manner. Some men

are quiet, others outspoken; some speak in generalities, others give specific commands. As much as you might like to have a husband with a different leadership style, you married this man as he was at the altar. Again, accept him as he is. Trust God to use your husband in your life as He sees fit!

A final word on desiring a godly husband—*don't spend so much time wishing for what you don't have that you forget to appreciate what God has given to you.* Right now, choose to appreciate and love your husband for who he is— and ask God for His help to be the understanding woman of faith God has called you to be.

Activity: If you've been struggling with the issue of expecting too much from your husband, especially spiritually, take a few moments to talk to God about the situation. I pray you will know God's heart on this issue. After you pray, you may want to write a letter to your husband, expressing your complete acceptance of the man he is right now and your love for him. (Remember that you are accepting and loving the person, not the things he does right or wrong.) Release him from your past expectations and tell him again that you love him. If this seems too difficult at the moment, come back to this activity when you are able, by God's grace.

The bottom line is this: God meets our deepest core needs. He alone is all we truly need. In my marriage, I had to come to the realization that Rich's lack of spirituality was not my responsibility, nor did it force me into a spiritually needy state. As it turns out, I have come to realize the blessing of being thrust into an intensely personal relationship with Jesus Christ because I didn't have my husband to fall back on! Certainly, to fellowship around God's Word and in His presence with the man I love would be what God's original design for marriage entails . . . but it is not *essential* to my spiritual survival.

Do not be tricked into thinking anything or anyone can take the place of a personal, one-on-one relationship with God. Ultimate fulfillment of soul and spirit is the result of a vital connection to God Himself, without which we remain basically needy, despite all of the other people and things in our lives.

O God,

Be the husband of my heart. I turn to You for my completeness. I empty myself of all longings, desires, and dreams. Fill me to overflowing with Your presence and peace.

Be Part of
the Solution

"*My* husband hasn't gone out of his way to do anything special for me since the day we were married. In fact,"
Angie confided in a friend, "when we were dating he
seemed like a sensitive and caring guy, but now . . . he's almost a different person. The honeymoon's over! He doesn't
want me to work, so I can stay home with the kids, but then
he complains I don't do anything! Well, he's not pleasing me
either. I have needs, too."

After her friend asked her what kinds of things she'd do
if she could go back to school or start a new job, Angie surprised both of them by saying she would love to take some
classes in flower arranging and interior decorating. Extremely creative and a fantastic amateur decorator, Angie
enjoyed putting seasonal accents around her home, inside
and out. Christmas always gave her the greatest opportunity

to express her creative expertise, and the past few years several neighbors and friends mentioned they could use her help decorating their homes and offices.

"Why not call around to several community organizations that offer classes and see what's available in the near future?" Her friend's suggestion really excited Angie, who went home and made a few calls. Within three weeks, Angie had arranged baby-sitting, and she was off to her first class in interior design. After the six-week class, she signed up for advanced flower arranging. It wasn't long before Angie set up a small part-time decorating business from her home.

With her new skills, extra money coming in, and pretty things around her all day long, Angie soon radiated charm and elegance that came with a healthy dose of self-confidence. Her husband noticed and expressed pride in her and her new venture. The little bit of time away from her children gave them and Angie a greater appreciation for one another. And, because she was getting used to leaving them with a trusted baby-sitter, she felt comfortable going on occasional dates with her husband, where they reconnected their bonds of love and mutual respect for each other.

What kind of needs do you have? Do you need more security, money, attention, friendship, creative outlets, or mental stimulation? Do you crave someone to spend time with, someone to listen to you, someone to help you make decisions, or someone to teach you a new skill? Does your husband meet all your needs? Did you ever ask yourself if your husband is *able* to meet all your needs?

On May 26, 1984, I stood with my bridegroom, hand in hand, before the minister. I remember feeling throughout the service an awesome sense of "oneness" with the man I was marrying. I was his and he was mine, and it was our overwhelming responsibility to meet each other's needs from that day forward.

Soon after the honeymoon it became obvious that we had a lot to learn about meeting each other's needs. And for many years, neither of us felt as if his or her needs were being met. One case in point: Rich couldn't get any peace, because I talked so much. He tried to shut me up and shut me out. I felt unloved and rejected, but I couldn't stop talking. If God created me with a need to talk and Rich with a genuine need for "space," for peace and quiet, how could we meet each other's needs?

Even when a wife has a strong relationship with her God, she remains in need of earthly fulfillment from people, things, and situations. Marriage does not isolate us from trouble and need, but it can provide a warm and secure cocoon of mutual love that insulates us from the searing heat of pain. However, even the most wonderful and adoring husband cannot meet our every need in totality.

What can and should you do when your husband doesn't (or can't) meet all your needs? First, we're going to examine some possible reasons your needs are not met. Second, we'll look at what you can do to see that your needs are met while honoring your marriage and partner.

FIVE WAYS TO TURN YOUR HUSBAND OFF (AND FIND YOUR NEEDS UNMET)

1. *Nag.* Nagging is asking for the same thing again and again and again and again, often with a whining, selfish attitude. This is a surefire way to annoy and frustrate your husband. Nagging may give you the desire of your heart, but only if your husband is worn down. A husband in this condition doesn't have a lot to give. More about nagging and communication in chapter 16.

2. *Bribe.* A bribe says, "If you do this for me, I'll do that for you." "If you fix the bathroom faucet for me, I'll make your favorite meal for dinner tonight" may be a pretty good trade-off that is acceptable to both of you—even fun. But what about, "If you watch the kids so I can go shopping, I'll give you what you want in bed tonight." Or, "If we're going to your mom's house for Christmas, then we're going to my parents' for Thanksgiving and Easter." Bribes can be a form of manipulation (see next point).

3. *Manipulate.* Manipulation means you manage to get what you want by working the situation to your favor, often unfairly, using deception or

deceit. For example, a wife wants her son to play soccer, so she doesn't tell her husband about the opportunities for basketball and softball; she just shows him the paperwork for the community soccer team. By omission, she manipulates the situation to get what she wants. Manipulation controls another person, like a puppet on a string. Manipulating is subtly (or not so subtly) pushing a person's hot buttons or deliberately arranging circumstances to your own end. This is a selfish and degrading act in any marriage. Most women are very good at it, and most men are rather oblivious to being manipulated (or choose to ignore it). Therefore, to honor your husband, you must vow to avoid this selfish and degrading act.

4. *Miscommunicate.* Your request could be too vague. Men often overlook vague requests. They may not understand the need or, more often, may not even be aware something is amiss. Maybe you say, "Honey, could we go out for dinner tonight?" when you are really saying, "I need to spend some time with you, alone, without the kids." He says, "I would rather eat at home. I had a lunch meeting at a restaurant today." At this point, you need to clarify your need by saying, more specifically, "Then can I ship the kids out and make a nice dinner for just the two of us, so we can spend some time together?"

5. *Cling.* A clinging vine may appear beautiful to the casual observer, but it often sucks the life out of the host plant and does irreparable structural damage. This is a picture of the wife who feels incomplete unless her husband is by her side at every possible moment. An over-needy wife is a poor and selfish example of womanhood. God made woman strong, nurturing, and resourceful. He also made male and female as individuals. Be very careful that you are not smothering your man!

We are talking about your needs in this chapter, as well as those of your husband. Women easily fall into one of two extremes. Some always meet others' needs at the expense of their own (and ultimately they are often so stressed and driven that they aren't much fun to be around). Others perceive themselves as such needy, weak people that they can do little more than center on their own needs. Neither extreme is much good as a partner. God desires that you see yourself as whole, "lacking nothing," so you can sacrificially love your mate.

So how do you find satisfaction for these needs with which you've been created? Let me suggest five ways to do just that.

FIVE STEPS TOWARD BEING A LESS NEEDY INDIVIDUAL

1. *Know your needs.* When you do express your needs to your husband or someone who can help, you need to have them clearly identified.

I'm amazed to realize how many people have never sat down and written out goals for themselves. How can we expect to accomplish things without knowing the target? Making a list of basic needs is a similar concept. Sit down and inventory your life. Ask yourself questions like: What am I good at, what do I do well, where do I need help, and what must I work on in my life? Taking time to ask yourself these questions and search for the answers helps you become a more fruitful Christian. Not only must you know God and His Word, but you must also come to understand the unique person God has designed you to be. What do you need to become that person? What will help you be more like Christ and glorify God?

Since the previous chapter dealt with spiritual needs, think now of human needs. Examples would be companionship, a listening ear, creative outlets, success, time, money, things, friends, a prayer partner, opportunities to do a particular thing. The four basic interpersonal human needs are to be loved, to feel self-worth, to be accepted by others, and to be needed.

2. *Know whom to ask to meet these needs.* We need people. Because God created us with strengths *and weaknesses,* we are each insufficient on our own—no woman is an island. In the last chapter, we saw our need for the Holy Spirit to complete us spiritually. In addition, those of us in the body of Christ must compensate for each other's human weaknesses. As much as we may desire to be independent and self-sufficient, God did not create us to be alone.

Your husband cannot possibly meet 100 percent of your needs. For example, no one person can meet my total need for someone to listen to me. I like to talk. When I need to think through a problem, or when I'm happy or excited, or when something amazing has just happened . . . I *need* to talk! Rich can't possibly listen to every word I have to say. Furthermore, he doesn't want to listen to me chatter after he has put in a long day at the office. It is unfair to ask him to meet this need in totality. Do we need to discuss things together? Does he need to listen to my ideas, concerns, and thoughts at appropriate times? Certainly. But if I talk all the time (which sometimes I do), he won't hear the really important things I have to say.

I have already identified talking as a legitimate need. Now I must look around to see where God wants me to have that need met. Is there someone I could call or visit? Does someone need a friend or a counselor? Teaching, speaking, and good friends fulfill much of my need to be listened to. So now, when I appropriately share my thoughts with Rich, he is much more willing to listen. I've learned to guard my tongue, because I recognize that one of his greatest needs at home is peace and quiet.

A word of warning. In looking to others to meet some of your human needs, be careful not to go too far. Sex is an obvious need that can be met only by your husband. But the needs for companionship, emotional intimacy, and friendship have the potential to leave you vulnerable as well, and should not be met by men outside your marriage and family, except in friendships that also include your husband. Relationships and friendships (especially on the Internet) can at first appear positive and meet many of your needs, but emotional attachments can damage your marriage at the very core of intimacy. Be cautious and talk to a godly older woman about how to deal with this situation if you need help.

3. *Know how to communicate your needs.* Using the same example of talking, I can tell you that Rich and I have not always clearly communicated our individual needs to each other. When we were first married, I chattered all the time, and Rich would tell me to shut up. I was hurt, and he was frustrated.

After years of practice and a greater understanding of this concept, I wait to talk to him about important matters until the *time, place, and mood* are appropriate. This is a sign that I'm growing older and wiser—and less selfish. Often I will pray for the Holy Spirit's guidance and the correct words as I tell Rich something important. Knowing the best time and presentation for *him* is a key to getting what *I* need.

Also, be direct and clear when you ask for something. For example, if you need his attention, lovingly remind him that you don't just need him to stay at home tonight and work on the computer or watch something by himself on TV. Let him know exactly what would be beneficial to you. At the same time, give him room to suggest another night (soon) or a slightly different activity than you had in mind (but agreeable to both of you).

Another helpful hint has to do with presentation. When a need or an issue I must discuss with Rich has me tied in emotional knots, I sometimes get weepy and ruin whatever time I have with Rich by making him feel uncomfortable. To eliminate an emotional delivery, I've found letter writing to be a great asset to our communication. But I don't deliver the letter and run! We agree on a good time to have a discussion. When the time comes, I give him the letter to read, and I sit with him while he reads it. The letter provides my objective, concise point of view. When he finishes reading the letter, he can ask questions to clarify, tell me he'd like to think it over and talk about it in a day or two, or give me an answer on the spot. This has worked well for us, as Rich appreciates the time and thoughtfulness it took me to meet him on his level.

However you communicate your needs, think carefully about approaching your husband on *his* terms.

4. *Know how to find pleasure.* "But," you say, "I know what I like and what I don't like. What do you mean by 'know how to find pleasure'?"

Preconceived ideas of what we want often act as blinders to the really good things our husbands do for us and the really great things God is doing in our lives. We spend so much time wishing for what we *don't* have that we miss what we have!

A good example is sex. Women are stereotypically more interested in romance than sex. I've heard it said that men put up with romance to get sex, and women put up with sex to get romance. That can be a valid thing to do—put your sights on the intimacy and romance of the moment, if that's what you need most, and enjoy the time with your husband.

Fulfillment comes when we rediscover our *sense of wonder.* Do you remember the first time you touched a fuzzy kitten? Walking into your new classroom on the first day of kindergarten? The first time a boy held your hand? Glimpsing your newborn baby just moments after the birth? Wonder is the first part of the word *wonderful.* Wouldn't life be better if you sometimes looked at things with childlike eyes, enjoying each moment to its fullest? Wouldn't life be more grand if you looked for the good points, instead of dwelling on the bad or what is missing?

You can look at the cup as half full or half empty. The choice is yours. Let me encourage you to make the most of what your husband is doing for you right now. Be appreciative. Thank him for providing financially for the family. Thank him for being a great dad. Thank him for all of his strong points.

5. *Know and remember that your core needs are met in God.* Why is this, the most important point, at the end? And didn't we cover this in the last chapter? I don't want you to forget it. I want you to leave this chapter with this point uppermost in your mind.

Do you realize that all of your needs—spiritual or human—were understood and provided for before you were even born? Read these words from Psalm 139 that tell you just how well your Creator knows you.

> *O LORD, you have searched me and you know me. You know when I sit and when I rise; you perceive my thoughts from afar. You discern my going out and my lying down; you are familiar with all my ways. Before a word is on my tongue you know it completely, O LORD. You hem me in—behind and before; you have laid your hand upon me. Such knowledge is too wonderful for me, too lofty for me to attain. Where can I go from your Spirit? Where can I flee from your presence? If I go up to the heavens, you are there; if I make my bed in the depths, you are there. If I rise on the wings of the dawn, if I settle on the far side of the sea, even there your hand will guide me, your right hand will hold me fast. . . . Search me, O God, and know my heart; test me and know my anxious thoughts. See if there is any offensive way in me, and lead me in the way everlasting. (Psalm 139:1–10, 23–24)*

God knows you. He knows your human needs. And He will meet them—in His time and in His way—to give you what is best for you. He uses many sources, even your husband! Nagging, bribing, manipulating, miscommunication, and clinging are self-centered ways of looking for fulfillment. Start from a vantage point of being totally complete in God's love and acceptance, and identify your human needs. Then, look for a variety of people to help you meet your needs and learn to communicate those needs appropriately. In this way you can regain your sense of wonder and satisfaction.

> *Dear Father,*
> *Please teach me my true needs and help me look for Your avenues*
> *of fulfillment. Help me to trust You to supply every real need.*
> *Give me, once again, a childlike sense of wonder and faith.*

Enlist Encouragers

Angie is constantly doing laundry, running to the grocery store, making sure everybody gets to soccer games, piano lessons, and play practice . . . and the list goes on. Angie asked a friend, "How can I concentrate on my relationship with my husband and remember to compliment him, when he comes home from work and jumps right onto the computer to check e-mail and then surfs the Net half the evening?" She needs help juggling responsibilities, help knowing how to communicate family needs to her mate, and even help from a baby-sitter now and then. Angie, who is always doing for others, hates to ask anyone to help her. She doesn't want to be a bother. She finds it much easier to give than to be on the receiving end.

Meghan is married to an unhappy, unfulfilled man, who takes his frustrations out on her. Daily, he belittles her with harsh words and exaggerated expectations. She needs someone to help her see God's perspective on this situation and practical ways to deal with it. She has always longed for someone to mentor her, but the only people who have ever showed an interest in helping her were those who didn't listen, but just talked a lot and tried to fix everything overnight. Meghan wonders if there is anyone out there who will really listen, pray with her, and regularly encourage her to put God's truth in action.

Carla married a low-key, relaxed guy who always says, "Yes, dear." While many of her friends think Phil is the most gorgeous man in the world and envy her because he allows her to do anything she wants to do, Carla wishes he would act more like a leader in their home. She is just beginning to understand their individual differences, but she longs to know more and be the person God designed her to be in this marriage. She'd love to ask someone for help, but that would mean allowing someone to see her imperfections.

Wendy is just a newlywed. She went into marriage thinking she knew what she was doing, but now she's not so sure. One of her problems is sex, and she doesn't know where to turn for help. She knows Ted's first wife left him for another man, but she has no idea how to help Ted regain his confidence and self-assurance in this area of their marriage. She feels out of control and pretty helpless. But she's got to find some help for Ted and get this marriage back on track!

Peaceful Polly just keeps sweeping her concerns and frustrations under the proverbial carpet. She hopes that if she just bides her time, things will eventually blow over, cool down, or just go away. She schools herself not to get ruffled or let Kurt know she has been hurt by his cutting remarks and harsh words. She can't imagine discussing her concerns with anyone (except in moments of desperation when she calls her best friend, Ann)—she'd never want anyone to think she has a less-than-perfect marriage. After all, Kurt is a deacon. She'll just commit her frustrations to God and let Him handle everything.

No woman is an island. We all need encouragement from time to time. Who has championed you in the past? Who is a source of encouragement in your life right now? Over her lifetime, a woman needs a network of supporters and various encouragers. Sadly, few women recognize their needs, and fewer still know how to ask for help. Most wives just take what help is readily available and struggle along the best they can.

Years ago, very few people discussed the intimate details of their lives with one another—even pregnancy was hidden after the mother-to-be started "showing." Privacy was encouraged. People usually worked out their own problems and suffered through negative situations alone.

Even though discussing private issues is more acceptable today, many people still shy away from telling someone else about their problems. A primary reason is personality. The phlegmatic introvert may be too shy to reach out for help or too unmotivated to seek it. The melancholy wife, also an introvert, may feel guilty that her life is not perfect. When hurting, an introverted person generally withdraws into herself or at best reads books. The sanguine and choleric dispositions are generally more extroverted, more comfortable to share with others.

Upbringing or past betrayal are additional reasons people do not confide. In some homes, children are taught not to talk about their problems. Others have been burned in the past by someone who broke their confidence and betrayed them. In many cases, women keep to themselves, unwilling to discuss their burdens with someone else, even when desperate.

God tells us to "encourage one another and build each other up" (I Thessalonians 5:11). Does it not stand to reason that at times we need to be on the other end of that encouragement? Surely it is "more blessed to give than to receive," but from time to time we ourselves need to accept encouragement offered.

Webster says an encourager is "one who gives courage, hope, and confidence; one who supports." We all need people in our lives who will come alongside, who will teach and mentor us, who will partner with us in times of need. What can a person like this offer you?

Possible Benefits from an Encourager, Mentor, and/or Partner:
    promotes genuine growth in your life
    is a model/example to emulate
    assists you in setting goals, objectives, expectations
    helps you efficiently reach your goals
    provides biblical teaching, training, and counseling

provides an objective perspective
offers sympathy and comfort
holds on in deep waters
exhorts—holds you to the truth
motivates and offers accountability
provides prayer support
benefits other people in your life
plays a key role in God's pattern for your growth

Vulnerability, humility, and receptivity are integral to growth. We can find help when we open ourselves to each other and are willing to accept advice, concern, and help.

Although many books are available today concerning how to *be* a good friend and come alongside a person in need, very little has been written on how to *ask* for help when you need it. How do you know what kind of help you need, who or what can help, and where to find this help?

DISCOVER YOUR NEEDS

What do you want? Take an inventory of your life: family, home, husband, spiritual life, church, community, work, how you spend money, what you do for fun, whom you spend time with, whom you admire, what you laugh at, what you think about. Evaluate yourself in each area, and then ask yourself where you would like to be five or even ten years from now. What must you do to get there? What knowledge do you need? What attitudes, behaviors, and/or habits must you change? And what skills must you learn?

What is your personal dynamic? If you want help getting where you've decided you want to go, you must choose the right person to help you get there. To choose the best person to help you, you must understand yourself—your *internal fingerprint.* You don't need to find someone exactly like you. However, someone entirely opposite may frustrate you, therefore impeding the learning process. You can benefit greatly from someone who complements your personality and has strengths in your areas of weakness.

How do you learn? Ask yourself if you learn best by reading/listening, watching, or doing. Do you like to "think out loud" in the presence of another person or people, or would you rather mentally think through a situation in a quiet, undisturbed place? There are no right or wrong answers to these questions. However, the answers will help you find the best person and situation to reach your goals.

SEEK SOURCES OF HELP

The help another person gives you can take the form of information, insight into a similar personal experience, an objective perspective, clarification of thoughts, a listening ear/sounding board, sympathy, exhortation, accountability, prayer support, and/or advice.

God is the first place we should run for help. His Holy Spirit, living within each believer, counsels us, teaches and reminds us of truth, convicts us of sin, prays for us before the Father's throne, and more (John 14:26; 16:8; Romans 8:26). And God also encourages us by His Word, His people, and His direct intervention in our lives.

Sources of help abound, but choose wisely as you seek God's direction. Do you need the encouragement and accountability of meeting regularly with a church friend or Christian neighbor? Perhaps a spiritually mature woman or Bible teacher can help you study the Word of God and apply it to your life. You may need to turn to the guidance of your pastor or a Christian counselor on some aspect of your life or marriage. You can also take advantage of biblically based literature—but don't become a scholar who studies books more than she applies the truth to her life!

Carefully scrutinize people you wish to ask for help. Sometimes asking a good friend or a close relative for help, especially when you need objective counsel, is not a good idea. Sometimes we do *not* need someone to sympathize and coddle us, but someone to give us tough love, to firmly help us do the *right* thing in a difficult situation. Choose wisely, making sure the person is more interested in what God wants than what may *seem* best for you!

Questions to ask yourself when selecting a mentor, a counselor, an encourager, or a partner:

Does this person have a visible relationship with God?
Is this person's lifestyle consistent?
Is this person respected and consulted by others?
Does this person cultivate relationships?
Does this person have innate or learned strengths where I am weak?
Can this person relate to my particular "internal fingerprint"?
Does this person listen well, and is she able to diagnose my needs?
Does this person teach and counsel from God's Word?
Will this person keep my situation in confidence?
Is this person well connected to resources?
Is this person willing to take a chance on me?

When a friend's husband left her for another woman, I recommended she find a prayer partner for encouragement. She immediately suggested her sister. When I probed a bit and asked a few pointed questions, she got the message. "You're right. My sister would side with me and not necessarily help me see God's hand in all of this. She's so mad right now, she's ready to punch my husband's lights out!" She was right. Her sister was far too close to the situation and biased toward her own flesh and blood. My friend prayed about the situation and within a week made a new friend at church who has been praying with her consistently for several months. They are enjoying their new friendship, and both are feeling blessed by their prayer times.

Ask God for peace and conviction about contacting a person or obtaining a resource. You can also ask Him to touch that other person's life and prepare her heart for your request and need. God may even prompt someone to contact *you!*

THINK THROUGH *HOW* THE PERSON CAN HELP YOU

How do you plan to accomplish your objectives? We don't intentionally plan to fail, but by failing to plan we may not readily succeed. Come up with at least a rough idea of how you wish to accomplish your goals. Ask yourself *what, when, where,* and *how.* When you actually contact the person and get started, your plans may need to be adjusted—but at least they give you a place to start.

What kind of help do you need from this person? When you talk to her, you will need to clearly outline what you need and possible ways of getting that help. How could you conduct meetings with this friend? Ask yourself questions like these: Do I need to meet every so often, once a week, once every other week, or once a month? Do I want to meet in a home or at a restaurant? Or should we touch base by phone? Is there a particular subject I want to discuss or a book I would like to study, or should we limit our time to discussion and/or prayer? How long should we meet? (Having an ending date, even if you later decide to continue seeing each other, gives a sense of purpose, urgency, and closure.) What kind of help do you need from this person?

ASK FOR HELP

Start with one resource. When you feel God's leading to pursue that particular person, make the contact. Here are some ideas on what to say to a godly, older woman when you call her to ask for help.

Is this a convenient time to ask you a few questions?

I have a need for some (encouragement, accountability, prayer).

Would you have the time and be willing to consider helping me?

If the person says, "No, sorry but I don't have the time right now," you could ask her for a referral or recommendation of someone else she might know who may be able to help you. If the first person you ask cannot help you, do not become discouraged, take the rejection personally, or yield to the temptation to feel God let you down. He may have led you to ask this person because she will be able to connect you to the actual person God has in store for you.

If the person says yes or maybe, go ahead and tentatively suggest your plan. Then ask the person to pray about this situation and call you back in a few days.

Continue to pray for this possible helper.

SET UP GUIDELINES

Once the person agrees to get together with you, a few guidelines are in order. Three principles should govern your time together: Keep confidences (don't share secrets with *anyone*), keep your discussion practical and pertinent (don't waste each other's time), and keep your focus on God (don't philosophize; stick to God's Word and truths). On a personal note, I restrict my scheduled prayer time with my partner for prayer only. We use other get-togethers to socialize.

Other points to consider include the following: Remember to give as well as take. Show appreciation. Don't cling—this means you should not call or e-mail this person three or four times a week, disregarding the other demands on her time and energy. Save your requests for the times you meet, unless one of you has an urgent or emergency situation.

At the end of each session, you may find it helpful to review what you've talked about and decide on an assignment you need to accomplish by the next meeting. This lends purpose to your times together and encourages you to apply what you are learning.

Before you meet each time, pray for God's direction and an open heart.

APPRECIATE THE PERSON GOD BRINGS

Many people have played vital roles in my spiritual growth. Let me give you a few examples from the past several years.

My second-grade Christian-school teacher has remained a good friend throughout the years. I even call her by her first name, Donna. She was my sounding board, encourager, and prayer support during my student-teaching in college, especially when I was ready to give up.

Donna was the one I called, about ten years later, when I was desperately struggling to understand the changes in my husband, to be a good wife, and to parent my toddler. This dear lady agreed to meet with me for an extended lunch at a local restaurant every other week, just to talk through the things that were on my mind and heart.

The lunches with this godly woman proved a lifeline to me at the time. During the two weeks between our lunches, I would keep a little list

of situations that came up and how I dealt with them. We would talk
about the things on the list at our next lunch, and she would affirm my
actions and thoughts or help me see how I could have better handled the
situation and people involved. Through these times, Donna taught me,
listened to me, and loved me. She encouraged me and sympathized with
me. On more than one occasion, she rescued me from "the pit," and
taught me how to learn to climb out by myself using praise. She also
held me accountable for specific tasks and for the general responsibility
of becoming the woman God wanted me to be. Moreover, I counted on
her faithful prayers on my behalf.

As time passed, our lunches were needed only once a month, and
then finally just "on call." I am so grateful to this wise woman who
shared her heart, her life, and herself with me in this nonthreatening, "it-
works-for-us" manner.

Sandy, my current prayer partner, is another source of encouragement
to me. Our partnership actually began because *she* called *me*, needing prayer
and hoping we could pray together on a regular basis. For three years,
we've gotten together almost every Monday morning at her house (except
summers when the kids are home from school—this never seems to work
for us). I bring my notebook with my requests and praises already written
down, and we share our lists and pray. Our total prayer time takes a half
hour to an hour, depending on how much time we take to discuss our requests. This prayer time is a prosperous time of the week for both of us.
When we can't get together, e-mailing or talking by phone helps us update
our lists. We are very flexible and forgiving with interruptions, but we do
encourage each other to keep our prayer time a priority.

Another benefit of my time with Sandy on Monday mornings is the
notebook that I'm filling with answered prayer requests. I write my requests on the left page of the book. The next week, I fill in whatever answers I've received on the right side, across from each corresponding
request. Then I flip the page and put down my new requests. When we
meet, I also list Sandy's praises and requests in the back half of my notebook. As I now look back through all of our entries, I am reminded of
God's faithfulness as I reread all the things He's done for Sandy and me
over these past several years. If these answers weren't written down, I

could so easily forget the details! I also find it interesting to examine how, where, when, and even sometimes why God has answered the way He has—always for His glory and my growth.

Be careful not to share anything with anyone that would break a confidence with your husband. When I talk about Rich in a teaching setting, it is only with his permission, and I always try to present him in the most positive light possible. When I discuss frustrations about him with my prayer partner or a friend, I only tell the person how I am feeling or the general situation, not necessarily the details about what Rich said or did to make me feel that way.

We all need encouragers, but not everyone feels comfortable talking things out when the going gets tough—some people would much rather think things through alone or with God. But we all come to places in life when we need help of one kind or another. Begin now to look for what help God may be providing for you—perhaps it is enough for you to start by asking someone to pray that you will find the help you need!

Although some people are reticent to ask for help, others go to the opposite extreme. These women search out a myriad of doctors, specialists, and counselors until they hear what they want to hear. I had an aunt who went to a different doctor every time the current one told her something with which she didn't agree. Cleaning out her home after her death, I found no fewer than three shopping bags full of pills, ointments, and medications in her bedroom. She did not make wise use of appropriate helps or helpers.

Proverbs 11:14 says, "Many advisers make victory sure." Although we want to look to mature, objective Christians for guidance, this is not an admonition to keep asking people for advice until we find someone who will tell us what we want to hear. Pray and ask God to show you who can advise, counsel, or encourage you in your time of need. Listen to that counsel and allow the Holy Spirit to help you know the truth and follow it.

James 1:22–25 says,

Do not merely listen to the word, and so deceive yourselves. Do what it says. Anyone who listens to the word but does not do what it says is like a man who looks at his face in a mir-

ror and, after looking at himself, goes away and immediately forgets what he looks like. But the man who looks intently into the perfect law that gives freedom, and continues to do this, not forgetting what he has heard, but doing it—he will be blessed in what he does.

Regardless of our situations and stations in life, we all need help. At different times of our lives God uses different people to encourage us and hold us accountable. Besides the Almighty Counselor, with whom are you sharing the burdens of your heart? Are these people, their words, and God's truths helping you to make positive changes in your life?

> *Dear Heavenly Provider,*
> *Thank You for meeting my needs before I ask. Thank You for the myriad of people You've used to help, encourage, and exhort me in past times of need. Help me to reach out again, to You first, and then to Your source of help for me.*

PART FIVE

Dealing with
the Past

Dear Heavenly Healer,

Through the pain, I will trust You

to help me look into the past.

O God, please bring divine

resolution and reconciliation

to my heart, mind, and relationships.

Purify me as gold.

Release
the Regrets

$\mathcal{D}$o you remember the Old Testament story of the destruction of Sodom? Abraham's nephew, Lot, and his family were warned by an angel to leave the city before its destruction. On the way out, the angel commanded them not to look back at the city. The Scriptures don't give us a reason for this detail, but we can guess that looking back would have impeded their progress, weakened their resolve to leave, or even caused them to side with the people of the city and feel God's judgment to be unjust.

Lot's wife couldn't stand it. Everything she knew and loved was back in Sodom. She'd left her house and the furnishings she'd lovingly arranged to create their home. She hadn't had time to say good-bye to neighbors and friends. A mental check through her meager baggage brought no peace—she'd left so much behind. What would happen to her belongings? What would happen to her neighbors and friends? What was going on back there? Lot's wife could not reconcile herself to this unknown future without a backward glance at all she'd left behind. She could not release her regrets and move on without a peek at the world she was losing. So she disobeyed.

The instant she looked back, she became a pillar of salt. Can't you just picture her on the sandy, sloped terrain—her feet and lower body headed up the mountain and her head and upper body twisted around to glimpse the devastation to her home? She never moved another muscle. Never made another sound. Not even a whisper. Instantly, she became immovable, useless, cold, unyielding, dispassionate, and no longer a part of God's important plan.

We too can suffer and become useless if we spend time, energy, and passion on something that conflicts with God's plans for us. Sometimes that means we "look back" and linger on the regrets, pains, or even joys of the past rather than taking up God's call for our present and future.

My desires and goals took shape by about age seven or eight. I wanted to be a pastor's wife, raise a large family, and teach school. My present life does not reflect the fulfillment of those dreams. I have the choice to look at my present situation in one of two ways. I can look back, bemoaning the fact that I am *not* a pastor's wife, Rich and I do *not* have more than one child, and I am *not* a full-time classroom teacher. Or I can look ahead and keep going, realizing that I'm becoming exactly what God intended when He hand designed me for His plan. By God's grace, I daily choose to see my life as God sees it. Along the way, this perspective has demanded that I release regrets and expectations—I can't look back with desire.

RELEASED EXPECTATIONS

At one crossroad, I *chose* to release my regret that Rich and I are not serving in full-time Christian work. Since relinquishing this desire to God, doors have opened to a variety of experiences and opportunities to serve Him in ways I never even imagined. And past experiences I counted as useless and devastating are precisely what I've needed to truly empathize and minister to other hurting people.

For example, Rich changed jobs and careers almost every other year for the first thirteen years of our marriage. One of those experiments drew him into truck driving—over-the-road hauling with an eighteen-wheeler. After his initial training, he needed experience, and he started driving for a company that delivered coast to coast. Prior to this job, he had worked in an office, pretty much eight to five. Needless to say, our lives changed drastically.

With the new job, he was on the road for ten to fifteen days, and then home for two or three. While he was away, I operated in the capacity of single mom, handyman, and Mrs. Everything. When he would call (most times unexpectedly) to tell us when and where to pick him up at what particular truck stop, Becky and I would drop everything and run to get him. For a few days we would do nothing but play with Daddy (Becky was only about three at the time). Nine months later, Rich accepted a local trucking position, but he still made regular overnight runs. Again our schedule changed.

God worked all of these things together for His glory and for my good and growth—even in situations I didn't enjoy. Take, for example, experiencing firsthand the "single-mom" territory while still having a husband and complete family unit. Granted, I did not struggle with all the issues of a one-parent family. But that situation gave me a taste of frustrations, inadequacies, and difficulties single parents face every day.

Second, I *chose* to release my desire for more than one child. For years, we tried for that next baby. Where was number two . . . and three . . . and four? I wanted a houseful of them! If you yearn for a child, you understand all too well the feeling of hope that buoys your spirit when a period is late . . . only to have the bubble burst when it arrives and dashes your dreams for yet another month.

I am not omniscient, but God knows all. As I accept this fact, I turn to Him and ask why. *What am I supposed to glean from this disappointment? What are Your plans for me?*

If I honestly evaluate my life and calling, I wonder what I would do with more little ones! The issue is not whether or not I could cope or be a good mother, but what I would need to delete from my present life. I would love to have more children, but I am grateful for Becky, and also for the many areas of ministry outside the home to which God has called me.

And third, I *chose* to walk away from full-time classroom teaching to do the will of the God who knows what is best. From the first year that I taught sixth through ninth grades at a local Christian school, I excelled as a teacher. After my first teaching year, we moved. Over the next three years, I substituted, then taught fifth and finally fourth grades. We moved again. In our new town, I was able to secure another fifth-grade teaching assignment.

At the end of five years, my goal was to teach the same grade in the same school for two years in a row! Then I got pregnant with Becky. Expecting a child did wonders to diminish my goal of teaching school. At last, I was to be given my very own little person to love and educate. At her birth, I "retired" from teaching to be an "at-home" mom.

Even before Becky came into my life, God developed another area of service pertaining to my teaching background. I've consulted and evaluated for home-schooling families for more than twelve years. Perhaps God will one day call me back to the classroom—but I'll wait for His timing and enjoy ministering to parents who need encouragement in the field of educating their children.

RELEASED PLANS

How could I possibly have known in college as I studied education that God would take my degree, knowledge, and experiences and weave them into an amazing pattern of opportunities to reach His people? You, too, may not know what God is doing, or perhaps why He has chosen to bring different elements into your life. But you can trust Him. "'For I know the plans I have for you,' declares the LORD, 'plans to prosper you and not to harm you, plans to give you hope and a future'" (Jeremiah 29:11).

When things look bad, we often look back and say "I wish. . . . " In essence, we are saying, "God, You don't know what You're doing," or "God, this situation is hopeless—You can't fix it." It is good to confess past failures. Surely, we should make amends when possible. And then move on—not looking back, but actively obeying God's direction.

Life is a race. Marriage is a part of a wife's course. Like Lot's wife, we can't look back or we'll lose momentum, trip over what we don't see, or stray off course. The best answer to keeping on track is to keep focused on the reason for being in the race—getting to the finish line. In the race of life, our reason for being in the race is simple—to do the will of God who called us. Focus on God. Look at Him, not the people running with you, the obstacles, or your own hurts or disappointments.

Let's examine the things we tend to look back to. What do we regret? You may be able to think of additional categories, but let's deal with unfulfilled or shattered dreams, mistakes, and hurts. How can we handle them appropriately?

UNFULFILLED OR SHATTERED DREAMS

Unfulfilled dreams could be the desire to have another child, a more attentive husband, a better place to live, a better standard of living. Shattered dreams are things like having your husband cheat on you, hearing your high schooler say she's pregnant, listening to the doctor tell you he did everything he could for your sister during surgery—but it wasn't enough and she's gone. How do you deal with situations like these?

Angie and Nick had only been married about a year when they conceived their first child. Angie miscarried the baby during the fifth month of pregnancy, and they grieved together. Nick got over the loss and returned to life more quickly and with less emotional upset than she did. Nick tried to draw Angie out of her shell by telling her to "get over it—let's have another baby." In response, quiet, reserved Angie buried the emotions she had not yet dealt with, along with animosity toward Nick for being pushy and unfeeling.

Whenever we lose anything, we grieve to some extent or another. In these years since Rich turned from God, I have grieved the loss of our spiritual unity. It is dead; I cannot have it anymore (at this time), and I've wept, raged, and mourned over it. As we grieve, we also need to find the comfort *God* offers through a relationship with Him, His Word, and His people.

A helpful way to deal with unfulfilled dreams is to symbolically and tangibly release them. Write the dream(s) on a piece of paper. In prayer, give this thing to God. Then burn the paper in a safe place and watch the smoke take your anger with it into the heavens. Note the day, date, and place, so you can mentally return and replay this scene when you are tempted to fixate on this disappointment.

MISTAKES

No one likes to make mistakes. But a wise person learns from her mistakes. People are usually in one of two camps when making mistakes. The first type acts impulsively, gets a lot done, and makes some mistakes along the way. The second type is more cautious, makes fewer mistakes, and produces far less—but almost perfect—work. Neither type of person is right, or wrong, just different.

It is not the mistakes we make that count; it is how we handle them. We can *learn* to appreciate the value and benefit of mistakes. We must learn that although mistakes come with consequences, eventually "this too shall pass." Ask yourself, "Will this really matter in three months?" If the answer is yes, this is a *real* problem, needing thought, counsel, external support, and daily prayer for God's wisdom (James 1:5).

Learn from the past—don't keep making the same mistakes over and over. Even more important, don't dwell on the negatives and allow them to pull you down. Satan would love to defeat you—don't let him! If the mistake is too big to face alone, call a friend for prayer, help, and encouragement.

God uses many methods to help us learn, because He wants us to grow. Sherry Hart, a Sunday school teacher at the Oley church where Rich was a youth pastor, taught me a valuable lesson on the persistence of God. If He wants you to learn something, He'll keep after you until you learn it. "So girls, resign yourself to learning the first time," Sherry said, "so He doesn't have to send more lessons!" I've never forgotten this great advice and often think about her words when I want to sulk or whine, instead of taking advantage of the mistake or other learning tool.

Melancholy people are particularly susceptible to the crushing impact of a mistake. The need to be perfect and have an ordered world causes them to be cautious by nature. Because they are careful not to make mistakes, any error makes them feel like a total failure. When I evaluate for a home-school child who has melancholy tendencies, I always counsel the parents to help the child learn the value of mistakes and see them as friends, rather than personal failures.

In handling mistakes, we sometimes need to apologize for them, but we always need to get up and keep going, never looking back, trying again and again until we get it right.

HURTS

Hurts we receive from other people also cause regrets in our lives. Every time we see the guilty party, the wound is reopened. How can we deal with hurts, especially those caused by people who don't care, don't realize, or—even worse—intentionally caused them? Is it possible to forgive?

Did God forgive you? Do you realize that *you* put God's Son, Jesus, on the cross? Yet Jesus still willingly died for *your* sins. "God so loved the *world*" (John 3:16, italics added), but "he calls his own sheep *by name*" (John 10:3, italics added).

To all who confess the need for salvation, God forgives *all* sin—past, present, and those sins yet to be committed. With God's attitude of forgiveness toward you, you *can* forgive those who have hurt you. You can see people who hurt, frustrate, and disappoint you as people who are hurting. You are able to feel compassion for them. You can learn not to take their attacks personally, but as an expression of something wrong in their own lives. This is true freedom from hurt.

Handling hurt with a godly, forgiving attitude doesn't always ensure there won't be bleak moments. We are human, after all. In times of distress, we must seek God's comfort. Read the Psalms, sing songs, and think on positive things.

Resolve to turn your back on the past. Press on. Look ahead. Don't look back like Lot's wife! Give every lost dream, every frustrating mistake, and every aching hurt to Jesus.

We cannot change anyone but ourselves. You cannot change your husband. But you can learn appropriate responses to the emotions he triggers within you. You can find joy in the positive aspects of your marriage. As you learn to react in godly, wise, loving ways, your heart will heal and grow strong . . . strong enough to sing again.

During my father-in-law's last months of a lengthy illness that culminated in death, he could often be heard quoting, "Pain is inevitable; misery is optional!" He chose to press on, look ahead, and await his reunion with his Savior. At the end, he rallied seconds before his death, looked toward the ceiling with a shining face, and said, "I see You there, and I'm coming."

Oh, that we all might relinquish our unfulfilled and shattered dreams, mistakes, and hurt to the God who can work even the bad and sad things to our advantage and His glory! Are you ready to pack up the cherished memories and hard-won lessons of the past, leaving everything else behind, and move forward into the present and future?

"Therefore, since we are surrounded by such a great cloud of witnesses, let us throw off everything that hinders and the sin that so easily entangles, and let us run with perseverance the race marked out for us" (Hebrews 12:1).

The only things we bring with us from the past should be cherished memories and lessons learned.

A Note from Nancy

Giving you the idea that problems of the past can magically disappear from your life and consciousness at the snap of your fingers would be a grave injustice. Oh, no, my friend. Some injuries take years to work through, and many leave scars that last forever. However, when wounds are treated properly, pain lessens and in many cases goes away. The key is a willingness to go deep enough to remove the foreign matter, and then continue through a complete healing process. Just as an improperly treated physical wound can become infected, so the festering of an internal problem affects the spiritual and emotional health of the whole person. God is a most capable and willing Master Physician and Healer. Whatever area of your life needs attention, God is able to supply the needed remedy—whether it be in the form of a Christian counselor, pastor, or godly woman. Also, give yourself plenty of time to recover and regain strength before going further in this book.

To "Let Go" Takes Love
(Adapted; Author Unknown)

*To let go does not mean to stop caring; it means that I can't live someone else's life
for him.*

To let go is not to cut myself off; it is to realize that I can't control another.

To let go is not to enable, but to allow learning from natural consequences.

To let go is to admit powerlessness, which means the outcome is not in my hands.

*To let go is not to try to change or blame another; it is to be responsible for myself in
that situation.*

To let go is not to care for, but to care about.

*To let go means I want what God wants in the situation, not what I think is best
for me or the other person.*

To let go is not to fix, but to be supportive.

To let go is not to judge, but to allow another to be a human being.

*To let go is not to be in the middle arranging all the outcomes, but to allow others to
effect their own lives.*

To let go is not to be protective; it is to permit another to face reality.

To let go is not to deny, but to accept.

*To let go is not to nag, scold, or argue, but instead to search out my own shortcom-
ings and to correct them.*

*To let go is not to adjust everything to my desires, but to take each day as it comes
and to cherish the good in it.*

*To let go is not to criticize or regulate anyone else's life, but to do my best to become
all that I can be.*

To let go is not to regret the past, but to grow and to live for the future.

To let go is to fear less and to love more.

To let go is to hug someone, but not hold him so closely he is crushed or smothered.

*To let go is to give a person or a situation to God, who is the only One who can
work everything together for our good and His glory.*

Dear Teacher,
Show me what I'm holding on to. Pry my fingers off and take it
away. Help me let go and trust You to work everything—past,
present, and future—into Your perfect plan.

Get Through
Grief

Have you heard one or more of these statements
from your husband?

- "I told you last Christmas I'm done visiting your par-
  ents. Take the kids, but leave me home. I just can't
  stand your family!"
- "I guess I'm just not a very romantic guy. You'll have
  to get used to it."
- "So I look at pornography every once in a while.
  What's the big deal?"
- "I'm really sick of hearin' the same thing Sunday after
  Sunday. Take the kids to church if you want. I told
  Jack I'd meet him at the golf course at ten."
- "Sorry, but I've got to work late again tonight."

Ever feel like you're always the one holding the short end of the stick? Has life thrown some mega-disappointments your way? Why is it that every time you turn around it seems like someone's stealing more of your joy?

I do many silly things to avoid pain. Sometimes I ignore it. Other times I run away from it. I make excuses so I don't have to face it.

Rejecting pain can be a grave mistake. Did you ever stop to think why God created pain? Pain alerts us to negative situations that need to be addressed. It helps us pinpoint problem areas. When we reject pain, we could also be forfeiting the healing we desperately need.

With any type of painful loss, we experience *grief.* Consciously or unconsciously we travel through a series of stages when we grieve over a loss. Take a look at the losses in your own life, and see if you can track where you are in the grief process. Sometimes just understanding what we are going through helps us to complete the healing process more efficiently and effectively.

We each work through these stages in different ways and at various speeds. Sometimes a stage can actually be skipped or gone past so quickly that it is not easily identifiable. Not only do different people react in various ways, but the same person can experience a different path through grief with each separate loss.

STAGE ONE: SHOCK OR DENIAL

Rich's words that Sunday morning in 1991 stunned me. "My prayers are hitting the ceiling. I can't feel or see God anymore. I'm sorry, Nancy, but I'm not going to church with you and sit there like a hypocrite. Give me some time to think this through."

I was devastated. I took Becky to church that morning, but I don't remember what the pastor spoke about or any details of the day. I don't recall much of what happened for several weeks after that Sunday morning. Shock took the wind out of my sails. I wanted to deny the whole thing. I remember thinking, over and over again, *This can't be happening to us.* My mind had been going in an entirely different direction. Oh, so quickly my life and plans came to a screeching halt.

Have you ever experienced a loss so shocking it paralyzed you? Have you tried to deny the situation, deny the facts, hoping you'll wake up and find it was all a bad dream? How do you cope? The practical answer is to keep moving forward. Go through the motions, fill your days with ordinary activities, and keep busy until you reach the point where you can think clearly once again.

During this numbing time, God asks us to keep Him in focus and press on. This prevents us from withdrawing or withering under the weight of grief. Through this stage we must cling to two specific aspects of the character of God: His great strength and His unshakable love. When we trust the hand and heart of God, He takes us through one crisis-filled day at a time.

"'I know the plans I have for you,' declares the LORD, 'plans to prosper you and not to harm you, plans to give you hope and a future'" (Jeremiah 29:11). "For nothing is impossible with God" (Luke 1:37). The Lord God Almighty says, "I have loved you with an everlasting love" (Jeremiah 31:3).

STAGE TWO: RELIEF, CATHARSIS, BLAME, OR ANGER

After the shock wore off, I began to gather my bones of contention and pile them at Rich's feet. I was more than ready to blame him for *all* our problems, because I saw him as the one who was in the wrong. After all, he was backing away from God—how much more in error can you be? I figured our problems belonged to Rich—he should take the responsibility for them. And I displayed pride in myself for the way I was holding up under these horrible circumstances.

Blame and self-righteousness goes the whole way back to the Garden of Eden: the first attempt to "save face." God wants us to own up to our own problems, however painful, deal with them, and keep moving on.

To stay in this stage spells destruction. Proverbs 19:3 says, "A man's own folly ruins his life, yet his heart rages against the LORD." Adam first raged against God, blaming Him for bringing Eve into his life. Why do we blame God for our own problems, mistakes, and shortcomings? I think the bottom line is we don't want to be wrong. We refuse to confess (admit we are wrong); we harden our hearts against God, which is *dangerous.*

God understands anger because He created our emotions. However, He warns us, "In your anger do not sin" (Ephesians 4:26). How is it possible to be angry without sinning? The key is found in where you direct your anger. Are you directing your wrath toward the *person* who hurt you, or toward the action committed? I've realized over time that I can love Rich but hate something he does or the way he says it. With this response, my frustration is directed at a thing, not a person—and my relationship is not broken.

STAGE THREE: DEPRESSION, ANXIETY, OR GUILT

I'm a guilt magnet. Are you? If there's a problem in my world, I usually feel like it's probably my fault—or I'm at least indirectly responsible. Eventually, I began to feel guilty about heaping the blame on Rich. After all, my parents had taught me that "it takes two to tango," and a broken marriage is hardly ever only one person's fault. So now, to assuage my guilt, I shifted back to myself as much blame as possible, which only left me feeling anxious and depressed. Now, as I looked at myself in the mirror, I saw what a pitiful person I'd become and wondered how soon Rich would leave me.

In this stage, a person can become overly exhausted or unable to concentrate and make decisions. Sickness can even result from the depression and anxiety. You may feel guilt for things you feel you should have said, for not loving enough, or for not doing something you think may have changed the situation. This guilt can eat you up inside.

God's Word addresses the futility of these thoughts by saying, "Do not be anxious about anything, but in everything, by prayer and petition, with thanksgiving, present your requests to God. And the peace of God, which transcends all understanding, will guard your hearts and your minds in Christ Jesus" (Philippians 4:6–7). In addition to knowing these truths, we often need a counselor, pastor, or friend to help us understand, apply, and practice them.

STAGE FOUR: FACING REALITY

Standing with the rest of the congregation, I just couldn't push the words of the hymn past the thickness in my throat. Oh, why couldn't I stop crying? For months and months, I remained in this fourth stage. A friend's gentle touch would start my tears. Sitting in Sunday school and watching the man in front of me put his arm around his wife or take her hand to pray just about undid me. The first time I sat in choir while we practiced "Trust His Heart," I had to excuse myself to finish crying in the restroom.

The reason I couldn't sing the words was not that I didn't believe God was at work in my situation, but because I did. I was beginning to face the reality of my present situation, and I believed God's truth, His sovereign plan for me, and His faithfulness—*but I still hurt.* I continued to cry buckets of tears.

When we hurt, sometimes we don't need answers as much as we need someone to hold us while we cry and listen to the anguish of our hearts. Gradually, as God works in our hearts, our grief mellows to sadness and infiltrates every aspect of our lives. And as we continue to live and participate in the living going on around us, God pours a balm over our heart and healing occurs.

SURVIVAL TIPS FOR FACING REALITY:

• Do take responsibility for yourself.	Don't blame yourself for others' problems.
• Do express your feelings.	Don't clam up around people.
• Do accept help from others.	Don't feel guilty when accepting help.
• Do reach out to others.	Don't withdraw into your own pain.
• Do give yourself time.	Don't expect too much from yourself too soon.
• Do know God is with you.	Don't believe Satan's lies.
• Do get rest, eat well, set priorities.	Don't become a couch potato.
• Do rest when you grow weary.	Don't sleep your days away.
• Do reflect on past memories.	Don't wallow.
• Do get on with life's details.	Don't allow your life to come to a standstill.

STAGE FIVE: FULL ACCEPTANCE OF THE FACTS

Seven years to the month after Rich's Sunday morning announcement, I attended a writer's conference with the first draft of this book. When an editor reading my manuscript asked how long ago my husband walked away from God, I answered seven years. She nodded and smiled. "Seven is the biblical number of completion, perfection. It seems to me God has completed a good work in you that is ready to share." For the first time in years, I looked back with a perspective that saw a piece of God's "big picture," a portion of God's handiwork, some of His plan and purpose.

Although I am certainly not complete in every way, the grief is gone. Reigning in my heart is a sense of acceptance—a settled everything-is-going-to-be-OK feeling that I know comes from God Himself. Joy has replaced the tears. And hope springs eternal that one day God may bring Rich back to Himself and rekindle our spiritual oneness.

We know we've come full circle when we can praise God for the trial we've faced, when we can find elements of our situation that are good and praiseworthy, when we can see God's sovereign hand in the painful past.

Realistically, no one escapes pain and loss. Regardless of the size and significance of our loss, we must work through the grief process. The key to shortening the roller-coaster ride is achieving balance in our lives. "Balance exists only as we learn to trust God's judgment, rely on His strength, and continue in our walk. When we are trusting, relying, and continuing, life's circumstances will be unable to paralyze us."[1]

"Let your eyes look straight ahead, fix your gaze directly before you. Make level paths for your feet and take only ways that are firm" (Proverbs 4:25–26). "Let us fix our eyes on Jesus, the author and perfecter of our faith" (Hebrews 12:2).

Dear Father of Compassion and Comfort,
I give up trying to deal with disappointment on my own. I come into
Your presence, ready—by Your grace—to face and accept reality.
Thank You for Your comfort and hope of a brighter tomorrow.

Focus on Forgiveness

"Hello . . . Nancy?"

I cradled the phone between my shoulder and ear, wiping my hands on a kitchen towel. "Yes, it's me."

"This is Carol, from your Tuesday night class." She plunged ahead without waiting for my acknowledgment. "I'm really sorry, but I can't come to class anymore."

"I'm sorry too. What's up?" I prepared myself to listen for the real problem, assuming she would give me a list of excuses.

Surprisingly Carol cut immediately to the heart of the matter. "I couldn't handle last night's lesson on forgiveness. I just can't do it. And it seems silly to continue from here." I heard her sigh. "I'm sorry," she said again.

"Do you want to talk about it?" I hoped she would.

After a moment, she began. "Last night in our class, I

couldn't participate with the other women who were giving God their lists of hurts and dislikes about their husbands. And, well . . . I just can't let my hurts go." Her last sentence was punctuated with a small sob.

"Tell me why you feel that way."

She took a deep breath. "I'm afraid if I let go of all the things that I'm holding between me and my husband right now, I'll be . . . vulnerable." She struggled to explain herself. "It's almost as if I'm protecting myself with this list of stuff Chuck's done. I feel like if I give it up, he'll think he can do anything and get away with it." She sighed. "Does that sound dumb or what?"

Sitting down with the phone at the kitchen table, I smiled. "Honestly, it makes a lot of sense, even if it isn't logical. So, let me get this straight. Chuck's done and said things to hurt you, and you are keeping a mental record of everything. Right?"

"Yeah."

"So what's this list doing for you? How does it help you?"

Carol paused and then answered, "It doesn't, I guess. But if I just forget about everything and let each thing he does roll off my back, he'll get the idea he can do anything any time he wants to. Then where will I be?"

I could hear the pain and frustration in her voice, and I hurt for her. "Back up a step. I know you know your Bible. What does God say about forgiveness?"

She gave a soft snort. "I know where you're going. God says to forgive everyone . . . for anything. Oh, yeah, just as He forgave us." She sounded exasperated. "But . . . how do I stop my husband from hurting me? How do I stop hurting inside?"

Softly, prayerfully, I answered. "Obey God." Silence. "He'll do the rest." More silence. "Do you believe He can?"

"Yes." It was not spoken with much conviction.

"Are you free for an hour or two right now?" I felt compelled to see Carol all the way through this critical situation, and my schedule was uncharacteristically free.

"Well . . . yes."

"Would you come here to my house right now? Let's go through the steps of the lesson together. Sometimes we need someone to walk with us through deep waters. I can't promise your husband's actions will change, but I can guarantee that the joy that comes from obedience will fill your life." I waited.

"Now?"

"Yes."

"OK."

Ten minutes later Carol arrived on my doorstep. Two hours and many tears later, she left with a clean slate and a clear conscience. The next week in class, she testified to God's work of freedom in her life. Two years later, she is still growing, still forgiving, still experiencing the joy of obedience. She'd be the first to admit that sometimes old habits still get the better of her and require prayer and active, obedient faith.

In addition, Carol and Chuck's relationship has gone through some dramatic changes. Carol's bitter frustration has been replaced with joyful, positive living. Most of the time, she compliments her husband on his finer points—and often he lives up to her compliments!

Just a few days ago, Carol sent me a note.

If I had given up that day I called you, I would never have experienced the freedom of complete forgiveness. Now, I keep really short accounts. Nasty words or actions from Chuck used to drive me crazy. Now, I use my shield of faith to deflect them away from me toward God, who's the only one who can help Chuck anyway! I seem to be able to live above the hurts (most of the time, of course). Thanks so much for being there for me that day I called. By the way, Chuck told me to thank you for his "new wife." I know you'll say, "It was the Lord"—and so it was . . . and is!

HOW DO I GET FREE?

In this chapter, we focus on how you can offer sincere forgiveness to your husband when he sins against you. Before we go further, however, let's look at both sides of the coin. Both husbands and wives sin against each other—because we all sin. And when the Holy Spirit convicts us and we recognize our sin, we are responsible to confess, to correct our behavior, and to seek forgiveness and restitution. You by God's grace can deal with your own sin appropriately. You cannot, however, confess or correct your husband's sin. In fact, you may often suffer from the consequences of his sin. Perhaps you are even a target of his anger.

Are you dealing with any of the problems I've come across counseling the women in my classes? One woman's husband threw her up against the wall when he got angry. Another woman, married twenty years with five children, had no clue her husband had an addiction to gambling, until he lost thousands of dollars they'd been saving for a new home. Still another wife is living with a man who justifies his addiction to pornography because he's at home on the computer and not out with a mistress.

Other hurts may be less obvious, but just as painful. Speaking to me after a seminar, a grief-stricken woman said, "I wish I had scars so people would believe me when I reach out for help. My husband's accusations and demeaning remarks cut through me just like a knife, but no one can see my broken heart and bruised ego."

Still others of us have petty irritations that sometimes seem insurmountable. Although "petty irritations" vary from person to person, here are some examples. He smokes, and even though he only smokes outside, his clothes and breath still smell. He bounces an occasional check because he regularly forgets to record transactions. Even though he teaches Sunday school and is supposed to be at church early, you and he are still always five minutes late getting to church. He tells his mother things before he tells you. He's not careful about what he watches on TV in front of your toddler. Even though these transgressions may seem minor compared with what we are tempted to label "big sins," every hurt and disappointment counts in this chapter.

What about you? What hurtful words has your husband directed at you? Has he pulled any punches . . . literally, perhaps? Are there weaknesses in his character you overlooked when marrying him, which have become tremendous obstacles in your marriage? Is it difficult to wait for him to make a decision, when you want to get the show on the road? Are you hurting because you need his arms around you, but he's not the touchy-feely type?

Whether you have a good marriage relationship or one that is holding on by a thread, everyone at some point or another gets upset with his or her mate. Each one of us is a human being, and therefore imperfect—yes, full of mistakes, inadequacies, and weaknesses. Sometimes we accidentally hurt another person; other times vengeance is employed. The more hurts and the longer they linger, the more the relationship suffers.

There was a time in my life when all I could see were hurts, pain, and frustration that I blamed on my husband. One evening after work, when Rich was late coming home, the thought of an accident crossed my mind. I was stunned and felt terribly guilty when I realized I would actually be relieved if he never came home.

Before you think too ill of me, let me remind you that many people feel that way at some point in their marriage. Even godly people. A prominent evangelist's wife was asked if she had ever considered divorcing her husband. No, not divorce, but—she admitted tongue in cheek—she'd considered murder more than once!

I believe the Bible teaches that divorce is only the very last resort, and then only in cases such as infidelity and abuse. "'I hate divorce,' says the LORD God" (Malachi 2:16). (Do note here God says He hates divorce, not people who are divorced.) There are no easy "outs" for the person who is disenchanted with her marriage and her spouse.

During the darkest parts of my marriage, I was ever so glad to have a child, because she gave me a very solid reason to hang on in what I felt was a cold and desolate desert of a relationship. No one else knew the depth of my misery. No one would have guessed at my thoughts or my feelings. I hurt, and no matter how hard I tried it wasn't enough. What was I to do with the hurt? How could I keep going?

You could be thinking, *You don't know my husband and what he's done to me. Your situation is nothing like mine. I cannot forgive this man. I'm still in the midst of a horrible situation he shows no signs of changing. I can't go on.* You are right when you think I can't relate to every situation—but I know who can: the God of forgiveness.

"My husband does not deserve to be forgiven," you argue. "He continues to do things that hurt me, and he shows no sign of stopping or even being repentant for his actions."

God does not qualify forgiveness on the basis of deservedness. He does not allow you to hold your forgiveness until your husband truly repents, says he's sorry, changes his way, and takes responsibility for his actions. The Bible says, "Forgive as the Lord forgave you" (Colossians 3:13). God offered us His forgiveness while we were still sinners, knowing we have the free will to accept His forgiveness or reject it. He can give us a spirit of forgiveness toward our husbands, even before they acknowledge their sin.

Do not underestimate God or the power of forgiveness. The forgiveness is as much for us as it is for our husbands! As a spirit of unforgiveness restricts all joy in our lives, so the freedom produced by forgiveness allows peace and righteousness to flood our beings.

Furthermore, forgiveness is a deliberate command from God. We ultimately have no choice. If we seek to please God in obedience, we must forgive everyone of anything. We must live with a spirit of forgiveness. It is a choice of the mind and will—*you do not have to feel like forgiving the person.* Feelings come after action; action is truth set into motion. Will you trust God to give you peace and righteousness in exchange for your unforgiving spirit? Will you act on your belief that God is big enough to handle these issues, if you will but trust Him and obey? Will you continue with this lesson and become F-R-E-E from your spirit of unforgiveness, resentment, anger, and negativity?

F – Face the Hurts

The number one thing you must do without delay is identify the cause of your pain and frustration as it relates to your husband. I want you to make two lists. On the first list write down all the things you don't like about your husband, things that hurt you or cause pain, and things he does that frustrate you. On a second piece of paper, I want you to begin a list of positive aspects about your husband. Think back to what first attracted you to him when you were dating and engaged. Add good things you've heard other people compliment him about (including things his mother says!). We'll use this positive list when we come to chapter 15.

Making these lists is meant to be a *personal* exercise in soul-searching and healing. I do not intend for you to share the negative list with your husband or anyone else (unless you need some professional help at this point, or the counsel and encouragement of an older, godly woman). The point is not to hide anything from your husband, but to deal with God about your response to these issues. Sharing the negative list with your mate at this point may very well antagonize or discourage him.

Identifying hurts isn't easy. Often we repress pain, which means we try to hide the problems and pretend they don't exist. Bringing them to the surface may require quite a bit of soul-searching. Vague disillusionment is also sometimes a problem—you may not like how your husband makes you feel, but you're not quite sure why he makes you feel this way. When making your list, be sure to identify specific *causes*, not just *symptoms*. (For example, don't write down "he makes me feel bad," when the real problem is "he calls me names" or "he never compliments me about how nice I keep the house.") It may take you a long time to complete this list. Naming each problem may cause you more than a little pain. But this is the first step toward healing.

As you look at the things that frustrate you about your husband or leave you feeling hopeless or hurt in ways no one can even guess, remember that God knew all about these things before you were even conceived. He created you with the abilities to overcome in every situation He allows within the flow of your life. He permitted you to marry this man—and His perfect plans for you, even in an unperfect marriage, include glorifying Himself and providing for your good and growth (Romans 8:28).

R – Remember You Can't Change Him

Admit defeat! This is one situation in which you can find comfort, relief, and strength in giving up. Changing your husband is not your job. You are *not* responsible for him, for his actions, or for his reactions. He is. One day we will all stand before God and account for ourselves personally. One-on-one. You and God. Him and God.

Now, read over your list of things you don't like about your husband. What can you do about these items? Nothing. That's right. *I am incapable of changing anyone but myself!* Reread this last sentence . . . aloud! You may wish to practice saying it, until it becomes part of your heart and mind.

E – Excuse Your Husband's Failures

Excuse each sin, weakness, and inadequacy. For our purposes, let's define the word excuse to mean "to release or overlook." Remember there *are* real, God-designed weaknesses and flaws from the Fall inside your husband. There may also be sins you need to forgive, unintentional accidents you need to overlook, and unrealistic expectations you need to give up.

Whoa! Are you thinking, *Hey, wait a minute, Nancy—are you saying I just forgive him and walk away from issues that need resolution?* I do not expect you to exonerate your husband from every past sin and offense against you, nor do I want you to permit him to abdicate his responsibilities to you as your spouse. I am not asking you to release him from all consequences of past behavior. *I am asking you to give up to God the resentment, pain, and unforgiving spirit you hold against your husband, produced at least in part by these items on your list.*

The bottom line is the forgiving spirit. Some problems need attention, communication between partners, and correction (we'll get to this in a later chapter). Other minor irritations and simple weaknesses in our husbands' lives we must simply live above. In every situation, whether it requires resolution or overlooking, *forgiveness comes first.* Whatever needs to happen is then carried out with unconditional love toward the other person and with his best interests uppermost in our minds and hearts.

A soft heart is the key. A soft heart allows you to let go of past hurts—to rid yourself of pain and disappointment. A soft heart even helps you overcome frustration about things that may still be happening. A soft heart abides in a righteous person who wishes beyond all else to love and obey God. A person with a soft heart does not harbor a root of bitterness about anything or toward any person.

"See to it that no one misses the grace of God and that no bitter root grows up to cause trouble and defile many" (Hebrews 12:15). A hard heart refuses to let go of anger and wants vengeance for everything unfair. Is your heart soft or hard today? Ask God to soften your heart as you contemplate His forgiveness of your sins against Him. And with a soft heart, forgive your husband.

In a private place, read aloud each line on your list, saying, "(Husband's name), I forgive you for (item on your list)." Don't read through the items like a grocery list, but take each one separately. You don't have to *feel* like saying these words. You need simply to be obedient and say them. Saying the words helps you process the deed and internalize the action of forgiveness. Saying the words is only the first part, though, because godly forgiveness comes with forgetting. True forgiveness says:

> *I forgive you, and I will not remember this.*
> *I forgive you, and I will not speak to you of this again.*
> *I forgive you, and I will not speak to others about this, ever.*
> *I forgive you, and this will not stand between you and me.*

I remember the time I heard our pastor read these statements that define forgiveness. I hurriedly wrote them in the back of my Bible, and they have been written on my heart ever since that day. This is the way God forgives us! Hallelujah. Oh, may God grant us the grace to do likewise.

Let me repeat, *eliminating your own unforgiving spirit does NOT release your husband from sin, consequences, or responsibilities.* This is about you more than it is about him. In fact, this forgiveness does not even require an apology from your husband who wronged you. Regardless of whether your husband cares about the pain you've suffered or is totally oblivious to it, you can be free of the burden of unforgiveness and hurt.

Just do it! If you are holding on to a spirit of unforgiveness against your husband in any area, you are living a defeated life. *Know* God wants you to forgive. *Forgive.* Then, *feel* released. Now your heart is soft again, pure and righteous.

E – Export the Problem to God

To *export* means to "ship out of the country." Now is the time to turn this list over to the One who *can* do something to change your husband!

First, tell God: "I cannot do anything about any one of these items, and so I release them to You, never to look back, never to dwell on them again, and never to let them stand between me and (your husband's name), by God's grace and because of Jesus' blood." I recognize this is a human impossibility, but it is possible in the strength of the Lord!

Second, burn or completely destroy the list. There is nothing sacred or mystical about the burning process. However, this tangible picture of the smoke taking the list to heaven helps clarify in our minds what we've done in giving this list to the Lord.

One of the most remarkable occasions of burning I can remember happened at my home with a young mother and her daughters (seven and eleven) who needed encouragement after their husband and dad left home for another woman. After the mom and two girls made their lists, forgave the dad, and gave their hurt and unforgiving spirits over to God, we burned their lists. We went out the back kitchen door into the yard, where they dropped the three lists, crinkled into balls, into an ordinary eight-by-eight-inch foil cake pan. We lit the paper, and the girls watched the fire with interest. I will never forget looking at the very few remaining wisps of gray ash, when suddenly a small gust of wind blew them right out of the pan—and they were gone. The pan was empty. The peaceful expressions on each girl's face told me they would never forget the moment, nor the lesson.

Third, note the place, date, and time of this event, so you never forget and don't have to go through it all again with the same items. You can even set up a monument as did the Israelites who so often looked back to significant moments in their history.

I'M FREE—NOW WHAT?

Some of the very issues and problems you listed, forgave, and sent to God will come up again. Maybe they are horribly regular occurrences. What then? Must you go through this whole cleansing process several times a day?

TRUTH 1: God Owns the Problems Now.

You gave the list to God. You no longer need to think of them as your responsibility. Therefore, the next time something negative comes up, think to yourself, *This is my husband's problem, not mine. God knows about it and is working on him.* Certainly you can ask God if there is anything you need to or can do to help with your husband's problems. In my experience, God usually reminds me to back off and let Rich figure it out on his own. So, I move on.

TRUTH 2: Your Job Is to Keep Standing Under Attack.

Our powerful enemy, the devil, will do anything to make us stumble and fall on our faces. God has prepared for you a "shield of faith, with which you can extinguish all the flaming arrows of the evil one" (Ephesians 6:16). Stand against him. "Put on the full armor of God so that you can take your *stand* against the devil's schemes . . . so that when the day of evil comes, you may be able to *stand* your ground, and after you have done everything, to *stand. Stand* firm then" (vv. 11, 13–14, italics added).

By using the shield of faith, you can deflect the pain and hurt from you to God (who can handle it quite easily), and in so doing you are resisting the temptation to carry a spirit of unforgiveness. Just as a soldier using a shield to deflect arrows or bullets, you will feel the impact from the weapon. However, the projectile does not wound, infect, or debilitate you. You remain standing firm.

TRUTH 3: You and Your Husband Are Fighting on the Same Team.

When you've forgiven your spouse of his sins and shortcomings, you are no longer working against him. His best and your marriage are the causes you champion. You are in your husband's corner, not on the opposite side of the arena planning to go head-to-head with him over your differences. This is a good place to remind you to love the sinner, hate the sin. Even when you don't approve of everything your husband does, you need to respect him. You are working together on everyone's problems, with everyone's needs in focus.

TRUTH FOUR: You Must Fill the Void in Your Thinking with Praise.

For so long, these hurts and disappointments have been a constant part of your life and thoughts. You released them today. There remains a hole. What can fill it? "Rejoice in the Lord always. I will say it again: Rejoice! . . . Whatever is true, whatever is noble, whatever is right, whatever is pure, whatever is lovely, whatever is admirable—if anything is excellent or praiseworthy—think about such things . . . and the God of peace will be with you" (Philippians 4:4, 8, 9b).

The most appropriate and obedient thoughts are positive.

When you look back and remember today's exercise in F-R-E-E-dom, I hope you continue to deflect the hurts off your shield of faith to God! You *can* live the victorious Christian life. You *can* continue to forgive, keeping short accounts, and feeling F-R-E-E of deep, wounding pain.

Humanly speaking, we cannot continue to love someone who consistently hurts and disappoints us—but with God all things are possible. God can help you release the hurt, pain, and regret. God can clear your mind of the past and help you learn to minimize present difficulties. God is our strength, a very present help in time of trouble. He gives us the peace and comfort and the hope to go on.

Know that I am praying for all of you women who struggle with burdens only God can ease. Hold fast. God is able. The God who sent His own Son, Jesus Christ, to die on the cross for *you* will help you forgive others.

Dear Master of Forgiveness,
Thank You for freeing me from an unforgiving spirit. I've released my hurts to You, and, by Your grace, I refuse to dwell on them again. Teach me, by faith, to deflect future wounds to You and foster a heart of forgiveness and love.

PART SIX

The Power of Healing Words

Dear Lord Jesus,

You were the perfect Word, sent from

heaven to heal me from my sin.

I want to be more like You.

Please give me a heart that

overflows with healing words

that spill out of my mouth

and bless my husband.

Practice Being Positive

$\mathcal{I}$n the first few years of our marriage, I wanted every vacation to run smoothly and delight both of us. I remember a particularly disastrous trip to Niagara Falls, when I had one set of expectations for Rich (of course I didn't know enough to let him in on them or consult him about them), and he had an entirely different mind-set about me and the trip. I felt rejected and thoroughly worthless because nothing I did seemed to please him. (I'm the people-pleaser, remember.) He just grew quieter and sulkier by the hour. And later—years later—I found out he thought he'd married a sulky, selfish, whiny brat.

Thankfully, since then I've learned a glorious truth: "This too shall pass." I've learned to live from one positive moment to the next and minimize what goes on in between! I can turn my senses on high and delight in the happy moments and turn everything to the "simmer" setting when life gets tough. It's sort of like riding the best waves and sitting out the duds.

Now, when I go on vacation, I enjoy myself and try to see that everyone else is having fun. However, when something comes up to make one of us irritable or unpleasant, I send my expectations and emotions into cold storage and try to make the best of what we've got. Every once in a while, this strategy backfires and leads me down the martyr's path, where I become a "poor soul, poor me—but isn't God pleased that I'm such a good Christian by sacrificing self for others." Yuck! *True* joy comes from truly sacrificing our own plans for others, *while* we find things around us to be thankful for.

At home, sometimes Rich and I companionably enjoy an evening. Other times, when one of us is moody or uncooperative with the other's plans, I try to shut down my emotions and go on autopilot. Sometimes I must force myself to stop trying to fix everything, and just put some space between us until we can get along again. In the past, I would have selfishly *insisted* that we have fun (never a winning idea), gotten teary or angry over the loss of my expectations, or felt guilty that I couldn't hold everyone together and make everybody happy.

I have learned to shut out hurt. Turn off my emotions. Turn my mind to the truth found in Philippians 4:4–8, which tells us to *practice being positive.*

> *Rejoice in the Lord always. I will say it again: Rejoice! Let your gentleness be evident to all. The Lord is near. Do not be anxious about anything, but in everything, by prayer and petition, with thanksgiving, present your requests to God. And the peace of God, which transcends all understanding, will guard your hearts and your minds in Christ Jesus. Finally, [sisters], whatever is true, whatever is noble, whatever is right, whatever is pure, whatever is lovely, whatever is admirable—if anything is excellent or praiseworthy—think about such things.*

Rejoice is a verb, you know! I can choose to do it, even when I don't feel the joy. (Hint: Joy is a *result* of obedience, not the cause!) So, I choose to dwell on the positive side of life and refuse to let the negatives get me down. You can do this too—for your sake and the sake of your husband.

PRAISING GOD DEVELOPS A POSITIVE ATTITUDE

Praise was one of the keys God used to heal my heart and give me hope. In *Dynamic Bible Study Methods*, Rick Warren suggests praising God for at least twenty things daily. What a great way to start each day! We can praise God for His attributes, creation, people, situations, answers to prayer . . . the list is endless. We don't have time not to praise God—the reward is beyond comprehension!

But what about a melancholy wife, who sees everything from the negative perspective? Can she, too, become a positive person? Yes, but it may be more of a challenge for this person. Remember: God would never command us to do something impossible, and the Bible clearly states in Philippians 4 that we are to rejoice! That a person's natural inclination is in one direction doesn't mean she can't *learn* to go in the opposite direction when necessary and advantageous. Practicing positives is a habit— something you do until it becomes almost as natural as breathing.

The apostle Paul encourages this habit among the people in the Colossian church:

> *Let the peace of Christ rule in your hearts, since as members of one body you were called to peace. And be thankful. Let the word of Christ dwell in you richly as you teach and admonish one another with all wisdom, and as you sing psalms, hymns and spiritual songs with gratitude in your hearts to God. And whatever you do, whether in word or deed, do it all in the name of the Lord Jesus, giving thanks to God the Father through him. (Colossians 3:15–17)*

First and foremost, praise glorifies God. Second, and beneficial to us, praise offers us the quickest escape from "the pit" and into the presence of God. Wow! When we practice being positive about who God is and what He's done, we join the angels surrounding His throne who are singing anthems of praise and giving Him glory, honor, and majesty. No, we don't actually transcend this world, but our minds and spirits are definitely lifted to a higher plane. In Psalm 40, David says of God, "He lifted me out of the slimy pit, out of the mud and mire; he set my feet on a rock and gave me a firm place to stand. He put a new song in my mouth, a hymn of praise to our God. Many will see and fear and put their trust in the LORD. Blessed is the [woman] who makes the LORD [her] trust" (vv. 2–4).

Praise produces a positive frame of mind. It encourages and lifts your spirit. It centers your focus on the God of the universe, instead of yourself or the situations around you. Sure, they still exist and you must deal with them, but praise reorients you and gives you a much lighter heart and a more hopeful spirit of confidence in the God who is incredible! And if we carry over the principle of praising God to also include daily praise for our husbands, we will really make headway in our marriage renewal.

> *Therefore encourage one another and build each other up, just as in fact you are doing. . . . Live in peace with each other. And we urge you, [sisters], warn those who are idle, encourage the timid, help the weak, be patient with everyone. Make sure that nobody pays back wrong for wrong, but always try to be kind to each other and to everyone else. Be joyful always; pray continually; give thanks in all circumstances, for this is God's will for you in Christ Jesus. Do not put out the Spirit's fire; do not treat prophesies with contempt. Test everything. Hold on to the good. Avoid every kind of evil. May God himself, the God of peace, sanctify you through and through. May your whole spirit, soul and body be kept blameless at the coming of our Lord Jesus Christ. The one who calls you is faithful and he will do it. (1 Thessalonians 5:11, 13–24)*

PRAISING YOUR HUSBAND
REPLACES FRETTING OVER NEGATIVES

Do you feel so disenchanted with your husband that saying something nice about him seems hypocritical because of all the other things you don't like? Been there, felt that! As a matter of fact, at one time I felt egotistically self-righteous because of all the things I thought Rich was doing wrong. I almost gloated over yet another sin I'd searched out. I was sure I was a poor soul to have to live with this man—and wasn't I amazing to be able to put up with it all! I must be a saint. All of his faults lifted me higher, so why was I about to encourage any good action on his part?

I also rationalized that I should not encourage Rich if he was choosing to live apart from God (and annoying me to pieces), nor should I compliment him. And then there were times when the darkness of our situation simply crowded out anything I could possibly appreciate about the man. Just dealing with the negatives made me so tired, I didn't have the energy to hunt out any positives.

Furthermore, my heart was becoming cold and hard toward Rich, and even toward God. In Hebrews 3:13, God warns us about the effects of negativity: "But encourage one another daily, as long as it is called Today, so that none of you may be hardened by sin's deceitfulness." *Encourage* means to build up, not tear down—be positive, not negative. I needed to change my ways—in a big way! I need to be positive with God and Rich *daily!*

I began to praise God for twenty things every morning. My world grew brighter. My heart began singing again. And the load lightened. But what about praising my husband?

After I realized I had to forgive Rich for the hurts, pain, and frustration he had caused in my life (and was still causing) and gave it all over to God, I was suddenly left with a void. A huge hole remained in my thought life.

I liken this concept to resolving not to eat any chocolate for a month. You know you are doing a noble thing for your health, but you can't get your mind off chocolate. You think about it when you get up in the morning, during the day, and all evening long. Your eyes zero in on the chocolate bars in the candy aisle of the grocery store, even though you've never paid much attention to them before. Everyone at the dinner party you are attending is eating some sort of chocolate dessert. It's winter and your kids are pleading for hot cocoa. Everywhere you turn you see chocolate. You've taken something away and created a void in your mind where that thing used to be. What can you do? Fill the void with something healthy. Get your mind off the offending subject. Concentrate on good things you will permit yourself to eat, go for a quick jog around the block, or call a friend and have a chat.

When you get rid of the negative thoughts about your husband, without replacing those thoughts with something constructive on which to concentrate, then hurt, pain, and frustration can creep back. So you must *practice being positive*, because positive things are what you need to fill the void created when you forgive and forget your husband's faults and weaknesses. The key is not only thinking about these things, but sincerely complimenting your husband on positive aspects of his person.

I began to do this. Every day I looked for something positive I could say. Something like, "That sweater makes your eyes look really blue." When he got home from work one day, I said, "Thanks for going to work every day and bringing home a paycheck that allows me to stay home with Becky." Sometime later, I reused that well-received compliment: "The way you provide for Becky and me is pretty awesome."

Were those things I said true? Yes. Were they already well-established facts? Yes. Did Rich really need to hear them again, considering he is a concise, nuts-and-bolts sort of guy? No, he probably would not have admitted that he *needed* to hear these compliments. But positive words encourage everyone.

Your husband may not realize he needs the words at first, and he may even laugh or scorn your encouragement. Or he may revel in your verbal love. Regardless of his reaction, keep on being positive in appropriate ways. Remember to encourage him on *his* terms . . . but *do* encourage him daily!

What about the wife who only sees the things that are *not* right about her husband, not the things that are good? How can she honestly tell him she's proud of something, when there are so many more aspects of his life she is *not* proud of? Wendy had a real problem appreciating Ted's tender love when he wasn't fulfilling the list of things that she'd given him to do around the house. "If he'd just put a little effort toward one or two of the things on this list, I'd think he actually cared. How am I supposed to snuggle up to him on the couch and believe he loves me, if he's been home for three hours watching TV and the kitchen floor hasn't even been swept?" Her friend Darlene responded to Wendy's question by asking if she would compliment him daily and not even mention anything on the list, for just a week's trial period. At the end of the week, Wendy reported that several items on the list were done, Ted got her flowers on Thursday, and she felt like they were dating again. One week. What does this tell us?

Hebrews 10:24 says, "Let us consider how we may spur one another on toward love and good deeds." Wendy, through her positive attitude, spurred Ted on toward good deeds. Indeed, this is how God intends marriage to work. Positive begets positive!

In chapter 14, you dealt with and rid yourself of the list of negative things about your husband. Now is the time to use the other list you created, the list of things you like about your husband, things he's good at, and things others appreciate about him.

Use this list of your husband's *positive* attributes to compliment him. Also hone your observation skills, and look for nice things he does, thoughtful words and actions, and any positive attitudes you can praise. At first, you may feel silly or "fake," or may not know what to say. But don't give up!

A caution. You don't want to go overboard, appear insincere, or sound like a "broken record," but you do want to make this exercise a daily habit. The whole exercise will lose its effectiveness if you are not honest and sincere. Compliment only what is a positive quality. It is far better to make a shallow but honest observation, such as "I like your tie today" than give an overgeneralized half-truth, such as "You're a great dad" when you feel he doesn't spend enough quality time with the kids.

Guard against using backhanded compliments that make him feel like a heel, such as "I'm glad to see you at least picked up *half* of your dirty clothes and put them in the wash basket." Tone and delivery are sometimes more important than our actual words—be sincere and without guile in your communication.

PRAISING YOUR HUSBAND CONVINCES *YOU* HE'S A GREAT GUY!

Meghan sat around the table with several girlfriends and became aware that the conversation had shifted to husband bashing. As she quietly listened, she became more appalled by the comments flying around the circle of women. Knowing her husband's faults intimately, she too could have shared war stories, but the Holy Spirit was tapping gently on her conscience. *This isn't right. We shouldn't be doing this.* Before she lost her nerve, Meghan jumped into the conversation with, "You know, I have to say that Keith has his moments, but I really like the fact that he always does what he says he'll do." She gulped and felt her cheeks turning red. "And I like the way he spends time with each of the kids on their level. Why don't we all share something we *like* about our husbands?"

Needless to say, there was a lull in conversation until another hearty soul picked up where Meghan left off and complimented her husband. Another and another of the women around the table mentioned good things, honorable characteristics, and fun facts about their husbands. Everyone left the get-together encouraged and joyful.

You too can benefit from developing a new habit of practicing the positives. As a matter of fact, *you* may be the one who is most encouraged by your positive words. You see, thinking of and saying positive things about your husband helps you believe in him again. You may be complimenting him, but you are hearing the words as well—and believing them. What a great secondary benefit!

Even if my husband, Rich, doesn't think *he* needs to hear my comments and compliments, even if he mentally tunes me out or thinks I'm "laying it on too thick," *hearing myself say the words has changed my mind and heart over a period of time and continues to keep me going.* I started listening to the words I was saying. I started believing in Rich again! My marriage turned around because I was *demonstrating* faith in God and love and appreciation toward my husband. And I keep it going in the right direction by practicing being positive. (It doesn't come naturally *all* the time, even to me—a sanguine.)

Let's look at how each personality type works on carrying out the assignment to daily compliment and encourage our husbands. The sanguine will have the least difficulty seeing the sunny side of her mate. She can most easily and quickly come up with a list of good things about which to praise her husband. She will enthusiastically embrace the idea and practice it . . . for a few days. And then other projects and newly embraced responsibilities may crowd out her good intentions, and she may stop encouraging her husband. Finding an accountability partner will help her stay on track.

Mrs. Choleric will only embrace this exercise in positives if she thinks it will really enhance her marriage—she has got to be sold on the idea. She will also have to believe in the truth that people need to be praised . . . and praised and praised. She thinks that once she tells you, she shouldn't need to repeat it a dozen times. After she has deemed this life change worthy of the effort, she will embrace the concept, adjust her behavior, and go to the top of the class. She simply must admit her need and *decide* to encourage her mate.

The melancholy wife will have the hardest time making the list of positives, although she was the first one done with the list of negatives. In her defense, being negative is a God-given aspect of "checks and balances." If you watch her closely, you will see that she hardly ever makes a mistake, because she thinks through every situation from the negative, avoiding most problems. Once she finally gets a few items on her list of positives, she then worries about other aspects of the assignment. How will her husband react? How should she phrase her compliment? What if he reads more into it than she intends or twists the meaning of the words? She may also worry about the possibility of causing a confrontation.

And the phlegmatic wife may finally get around to finishing her list in another month or two. She gets credit, though, for giving quite a bit of thought to complimenting her husband. Actually, she has practiced exactly what she wants to say so many times she's really not sure anymore whether she's said the words aloud yet or not. Maybe tomorrow she'll think about it some more. She would benefit from finding an accountability partner.

What are you waiting for? Go right now and find your husband. Remind him about a really fun time you had when you were dating or first married, or tell him how much more he means to you now that some years have passed. Or write a little note that will make him feel good about himself. Put it in his underwear drawer or lay it on his favorite chair. Or, if you can't bring yourself to say anything just yet, buy his favorite candy bar or a pack of gum and put it by his computer, in his sock drawer, or under his pillow.

The concept of practicing positive thinking and praise not only works, but the Bible recommended it long before people came up with the idea. Look at what God has to say about joy in James 1:2, "Consider it pure joy, my [sisters], whenever you face trials of many kinds." Yes, even in the face of disappointment, discouragement, and despair God reserves some joy for you. Can you find it? Have you developed an attitude of gratitude?

Remember that James says we must be doers of the Word, not merely hearers (James 1:22). We must practice praise. It is a discipline. Hebrews 12:11 says, "No discipline seems pleasant at the time, but painful. Later on, however, it produces a harvest of righteousness and peace for those who have been trained by it." God bless you as you train yourself to be obediently positive.

> *O Lord,*
> *I rejoice in You, most awesome God. I will speak of Your marvelous works in my life and marriage. I will open my eyes and look for reasons to rejoice. Thank You, O God, for giving me breath to praise You.*

$\mathcal{I}$’ve heard many women complain, "My husband isn't everything I thought he was when I married him." Or, "I was blind to all his faults at the wedding." I even had one lady tell me, "I don't need this class when it's my husband who has all the problems."

Early in my relationship with Rich, I attended a Bible study centered around the topic of becoming a godly wife. One particular week, the teacher made a point that women should not nag their husbands, but allow God to change their husbands if and as He saw fit. Well, when I see a problem, I like to fix it, even if it belongs to someone else! I know that tackling another person's problem usually results in stress, resentment, and frustration—for the "fixer" and the "fixee." But I still get stuck in the trap. Furthermore, I had previously thought that talking about problems—

whether mine, his, or ours—was an important part of communication within the marriage relationship. As I drove home that night, I wrestled with this issue of submission and asked God to show me His truth on the subject. I even boldly suggested a possible example He could use.

Life has gotten much more complicated over the years, but the simple thing I wanted God to change about Rich on that particular evening was turning his socks right side out. Washing and folding Rich's laundry was something I enjoyed doing for him, but I felt constantly annoyed with him for leaving his socks inside out. I allowed myself to be irked with the extra effort his thoughtlessness required of me. Before I got out of the car that night, I asked the Lord to "fix" Rich without my intervention.

Imagine my astonishment the very next day, when I took his socks out of the dryer and found every last one turned right side out! Later, it was Rich who brought up the subject, saying, "I really appreciate your doing my laundry, and it occurred to me that I could be a little bit more helpful from my end of things." He had no idea that he was part of a genuine answer to prayer.

Although my first impulse is still to be a "fixer," I often remember the socks episode. No, God doesn't answer every request to change my husband as He did this one. But I believe He answered me that night to give me a lasting illustration of this very real principle: Don't expect to change the other person.

Hopefully, by this point in the study, you too realize you can't change anyone but yourself. Regardless of this truth, we still try! Especially when it comes to husbands. In this chapter we will look at one of the worst things you can do to your mate—and the positive alternative.

Never Ever N-A-G!

Wendy nagged Ted. Every evening, when she got home from work and found him in the chair in front of the TV instead of doing one of the items on her checklist, she nagged. If you had asked Wendy what she was doing, she would have said, "I'm *reminding* Ted of what he should be doing." *Reminding* doesn't sound as bad as nagging, does it?

Nagging is a skill most people learn early in life. It happens when you remind a person again and again and again and again, perhaps with a whine in your voice and a selfish attitude in your heart. Webster says *to nag* is "to annoy, pester, or trouble with continual scolding, correction, or faultfinding." Effectively discussing a problem with your spouse is far different from day-after-day reminders and innuendoes that wear down and annoy the poor man.

The first place we experience nagging is usually in our childhood home. Unfortunately, many parents do not discipline their children wisely. With everything Mom has to accomplish by the end of a day, sometimes it is easiest to resort to repeated and meaningless reminders (moms are most often the naggers), when she should really take action and follow through on her initial communication with the child. More effort is required to work with the child, rather than to harp on the child with increasing volume and distress. So, we nag our children.

We also nag our husbands. Let's say your husband arrives home from work about a half hour later than usual because he got stuck on the phone with a client and then forgot to call home to tell you he'd be late. You scold him for being late the minute he walks in the door, and remind him about it five or six times during the evening. The next morning, you tell him three time before he leaves for work to call you if he's going to be late. And you don't even realize you're nagging.

Wives who nag husbands want them to change something about themselves, but are reluctant to trust the situation to God and often unwilling to discuss the problem appropriately. The result is a constant battering, belittling, and beating down that erodes a relationship. Nagging wears down both parties. Naggers expend too much energy and gray matter on criticism, and "naggees" either actively retaliate or passively defend themselves by escaping physically or mentally.

Every wife wants to change *something* about her husband. After all, we are all different—no two people think alike, act alike, or speak the same way. And we have each had many years to become the unique individual that shows up at the altar. Now we live together. I think he should conform to my way of thinking and acting, and he thinks I should be more like him!

Nick attracted Angie with his outgoing, vivacious, and fun-loving nature. Nick loved the way Angie listened to his stories, laughed at his jokes, and always allowed him to take the spotlight. After they were married, Angie became increasingly frustrated with Nick's happy-go-lucky attitude about everything. Nick was just as disenchanted with Angie's dark moods. Angie wanted Nick to have serious talks with her, but every time they sat down to discuss something, Nick would say something funny to lighten the mood. Angie would clam up, making Nick wonder if she was mad at him.

Someone wisely said, "Opposites attract, then they distract, and finally they attack!" We have to consciously let some of our frustrations go and practice being positive. Hey, wasn't that in the last chapter? Yes, but it is a part of all of marriage. When we don't practice being positive, we usually end up being negative. Negativity shows up in our attitudes, actions, and particularly our words. Unless we consciously speak the truth in love (see the next chapter), the words we do say resemble nagging.

Let's look at the components that make up a "nag": **n**egative words, **a**ggravating delivery, and **g**reedy attitude.

N – Negative Words

Negative words serve to tear down rather than build up. As a matter of fact, negative words can scar a person for life. My father had a brusque fifth-grade teacher who told him to read aloud to the class, only to make fun of a mispronounced word during his reading. To this day, he feels uncomfortable reading aloud to a group and often declines when given the opportunity. This story is sad, but sadly not unusual.

On the other hand, one compliment can make a person's day. A word of encouragement is an excellent motivator. Even hearing something negative presented in a positive light is more palatable than crititism.

There is power in words. Power to hurt or to heal, to empower or to humiliate. Even one word is too many at times when no words should be spoken, or when a soft answer is needed.

Have you listened to yourself lately? Are you using negative or positive words when you speak to others?

Try this listening test. On a sheet of lined paper, write down exactly what you say to your husband for the next several hours or days. Use a different line for each comment. Be faithful; carry the paper with you wherever you go and write down everything you say. When the paper is full, put it in a drawer for a few days. Then, go back and read what you said to him. What did he hear? Were your words negative *or positive?*

A – Aggravating Delivery

Aggravating delivery can be just as detrimental as the words themselves. The old adage "It's not what you say; it's how you say it" applies here.

Nagging incorporates a specific type of delivery that can be equated to the constant drip, drip, drip of a malfunctioning faucet. Have you ever tried to sleep with a drippy faucet in the next room? The sound is enough to make you feel you'll go mad! Furthermore, given time, the tiny drips eventually erode the surface of the sink.

Nagging does exactly the same thing to your husband. Your words come across as annoying, and your constant griping wears him down. Be honest. Which husband is going to be more fun—a worn-down, worn-out fellow, or a man who feels good about himself and his marriage?

The elements of delivery range from time and place to style, pitch, and loudness. What you say has better impact when you choose the right time, place, and mood. Your tone of voice is greatly affected by your mental perspective, your heart attitude, and your purpose in talking about this issue.

Go back to your listening test and ask yourself how you sounded when you said various things on the list. There is a world of difference between speaking with sincerity and speaking with sarcasm. How's your delivery?

G – Greedy Attitude

Having a greedy attitude means I'm thinking more about myself and my needs than about the other person. Not all, but much nagging originates from a self-centered, greedy attitude . . . a desire to get the other person to fix his problem so my world will be better.

When we are so wrapped up in another person's problem that we constantly bring it up, nothing gets accomplished. Ask yourself, "Is what I'm saying to him making a difference? Is it helping him or solving the problem?" Could it be that you are so zeroed in on that one problem that you can't see the forest for the trees?

If you made a list of the little things you'd like to change about your husband, how many of the items on that list, if changed, would make *his* life better—and how many would improve *your* life? Let's face it, most of the things we nag our husbands about are little things that annoy us: forgetting to put the toothpaste cap on the tube, leaving dishes in the sink when he could put them in the dishwasher, or not getting somewhere on time. Most of these examples could be considered differences of opinion. Maybe he likes to arrive sociably late!

Ask yourself, "Will this thing that I'm nagging him about still matter five years from now? Is it something that I really need to 'go to the wall over'? Or am I just being selfish and demonstrating a greedy attitude?"

WHAT'S THE SOLUTION?

Taking something away without replacing it with something else leaves us feeling unsatisfied. When you decide not to nag, you must decide what to do instead. Let me suggest that a positive alternative to nagging is *respect.* But, you say, my husband doesn't deserve my respect—he's got all these problems!

Respect is not an option; it is a command: "Let the wife see that she respects and reverences her husband [that she notices him, regards him, honors him, prefers him, venerates, and esteems him; and that she defers to him, praises him, and loves and admires him exceedingly]" (Ephesians 5:33 AMP, brackets in original).

James Dobson says:

The way we behave from day to day is largely a function of how we respect or disrespect the people around us. The way employees perform is a product of how they respect the boss. The

182

*way children behave is an outgrowth of their respect for their parents . . . and certainly, the way husbands and wives relate is a function of their mutual respect and admiration. That's why marital discord **almost always** emanates from seething disrespect somewhere in the relationship! That is the **bottom line** of romantic confrontation.*[1]

Respect is an integral part of marriage—a part of most marriage vows. Are you keeping your promises? Positional respect is possible even when earned respect is missing. God isn't going to hold you accountable for what your husband does or doesn't do, but He will judge you according to the actions and attitudes you demonstrate toward your mate.

How can you learn (or relearn) to respect your husband? Putting the emphasis on your husband's positive qualities is the first step toward honoring and respecting him. Appreciating him and being grateful for the good things about him begins to change your attitude.

REPLACE NAGGING WITH RESPECT

Start this process by learning to respect God. I've found that people who show little respect for people and things have no time or respect for God. Until we come to a point of being awestruck with the person of God, we cannot understand what it is to honor, esteem, and respect the Creator and Sustainer of the universe. In turn, we cannot correctly respect ourselves or anyone else.

In order to have an "attitude of gratitude," you must first have a deep and abiding belief in the sovereign love of God. He is sovereign; He is in control. And He loves us. There is nothing I can do that will make God love me more, and there is nothing I can do that will make God love me less. He loves me so much that, in His sovereignty, He always allows into my life whatever is best for me, what will bring me closer to Him, and what will ultimately glorify Him. I believe He loves me. I believe He has everything under control. I rest in His love and control of my life. I rejoice, praise, and thank Him for everything—large and small, the good and even the seemingly bad things that come into my life. In everything I will praise Him.

Once I appropriately revere God, I am free to see myself as His creation. He made me the way I am, gave me value, and then bought me back when I was lost in sin. He loves me and has an incredible plan for my life. In response, I need to respect, care for, and see myself from His perspective. *Then* I can love and respect others appropriately.

To replace nagging with respect, first I must respect and honor God as He deserves. Next, I need to see myself as God's valued child. And finally, I need to see my husband as a most precious person, specifically created by God for me, for our marriage, and for God's plans for us on this earth.

"But it's so hard to respect my husband," you say. "I just can't get past his faults." Ephesians 5:33 says, "Each one of you also must love his wife as he loves himself, and the wife must respect her husband." Note: Our respect is not dependent on our husband's loving actions and words. Respecting my mate flows directly from an obedient heart toward God.

Loving and respecting your husband is a process. Practice makes perfect, and each little movement in the right direction is a part of the big picture. Here are some steps to practice.

First, *decide never to nag again—from this moment forward.* Ask the Holy Spirit to set a guard at your mouth. Clamp it tightly closed and run the other way when you feel like reminding, nagging, calling attention to the problems in your husband's life. Hands off. Lips closed.

Second, *practice being positive.*

Third, *keep at it! Don't give up.* Nagging is a harmful habit that takes quite a bit of determination to break. But it is worth it and will have tremendous benefit in your marriage if you do not grow weary and give up. Susan Yates wisely admonishes us: "Respect is a habit that is developed daily in little ways."

DEALING WITH REAL PROBLEMS

Even though you can't change your husband, you do have to live with him. And there are times in every marriage when a wife is confronted by a very real and significant problem in her husband's life. How can you help your husband without nagging, but by showing respect, genuine love, and compassion?

When I was a little girl, I often fell and skinned my knees. My mother would do what she could to fix the problem—wash the cut, spray antiseptic on it, put on a bandage—and then she would distract me, to help get my mind off the "injury."

Mom taught me a wonderful lesson: When there is a problem, do what you can to help, then get on to the next thing. She did what she could for my knee (sure, it still hurt!), but she gave the healing process over to God and moved me on. She *didn't* constantly remind me to be more careful, and she didn't dwell on my klutziness—she loved me in spite of my lack of coordination. By the way, I'm still not very coordinated, but I don't often skin my knees anymore!

When you have a problem with your mate, ask yourself if there is anything you can do or say that will help *him* (not you) to arrive at the best possible resolution. Sometimes you could say, "I don't agree with how you're handling this situation. I'd like to discuss some ideas with you, if you are receptive." Sometimes you shouldn't say a word; your non-condemning, loving, supportive presence is enough to lend him the support he needs to battle this problem in his life. Other times, you may need to give him space, commit the thing to God, ignore the situation, and distract yourself—move on.

Finally, what do you do with a problem that you can't solve and that he shows no signs of being concerned about? For many years I sat in the car as Rich tuned the radio to a rock station. I would pray for deliverance, all the while tuning my own countenance to my holier-than-thou persona. My ears caught every word, and I remember the pity parties I held for miles and miles, wishing my husband would act like the dedicated pastor I thought I'd married. I would huddle far away from Rich, against the door, often pulling my coat collar up over my ears. I'm sure Rich got the message—nag, nag, nag. I was condemning him without even saying a word!

But didn't God expect me to shun evil? Wasn't I justified in my frustration at being forced to listen to music that I felt dishonored God? Shouldn't I let Rich know of my disapproval? Questions like these plagued me for years.

Finally a counseling pastor from our church guided me to the truth. From his own background that included rock music, he reminded me that Rich's musical taste is just a symptom of his hard heart. Treating a symptom is never as good as curing the disease. He went on to tell me that because winning Rich's heart for the Lord is the real concern, a small battle like his music is not worth *fighting* over.

When I actively stopped condemning my husband for the things that irritated and distressed me, I began to heal. Rich still plays "his music" in the car and at home, but God has given me the grace to ignore it (something I never thought possible). The different kinds of music in our home have allowed me the opportunity to help Becky learn to make godly listening choices.

Being told we are wrong can put us on the defensive. Condemnation rarely causes us to correct our behavior, especially if the speaker's delivery is less than tactful. It simply tears us down.

On the other hand, *love and respect build up.*

Can you really do anything to change your husband? No. Can you release your husband's problems to the Holy Spirit and keep your mouth shut? Yes. Can you focus on other things and get your mind off the areas you'd like to change? Yes. Good for you—go do it!

"Every wise woman buildeth her house: but the foolish plucketh it down with her hands. . . . In the mouth of the foolish is a rod of pride: but the lips of the wise shall preserve them" (Proverbs 14:1, 3 KJV).

> *Dear Father God,*
> *I release to You any dissatisfactions with my husband. Help me to focus on the good in him and to build up my house, rather than tear it down. Keep a guard on my lips, and help me sing Your praises.*

17

Speak with Sincerity

*M*eghan glanced at the clock on the dashboard as she drove the truck to the car wash. *Why am I doing this?*

The other part of her mind answered. *Because you've got to go to the grocery store anyway.*

And just why is a sane person going to the grocery store at eleven o'clock at night?

Because Keith needs a sandwich, yogurt, and an apple in his lunch tomorrow, and the fridge is bare. And out of the love in your heart, you offered to wash the truck on the way to the store, because you know his love language is "acts of kindness." You know, you could have said, "Could you please buy your lunch tomorrow? Today has been a little hectic and I'm out of lunch stuff."

It's a little late for that now.

You could have done the grocery shopping earlier.

Just when could that have happened? Maybe somewhere between finishing the laundry, collecting and putting out the garbage, visiting Sarah's fourth-grade classroom for their history project program, taking the kids to piano lessons, and dropping off a meal at the Larsens?

You know Jean Larsen really appreciated the meal, and she looked like the recovery from her surgery is going well.

That still leaves me driving to the car wash and shopping for groceries at a ridiculous hour!

Just think how empty the aisles will be—and no lines at the checkout.

You're hopeless! I just hope Keith appreciates his wonderful wife.

Next time, be honest and tell him your predicament—that the day was jammed, you don't have food for his lunch, and you are exhausted. He just may understand.

You're right. I've thought this before, but I don't do it. Gotta do it all—and can't.

Meghan has a problem speaking the truth to Keith. She thinks and speaks her good intentions, not the truth. She's the epitome of "the spirit is willing, but the body is weak." In this case, the flesh should have been a little more realistic. But Meghan is the eternal optimist and sincerely wants to do all the nice things she thinks of for all of the special people in her life.

Kurt came bounding in the door from the garage and grabbed Polly around the waist. "Guess what your amazing husband did today?" His kiss stopped any potential response. His eyes sparkled as he twirled Polly around the kitchen. "I landed the Hanson deal, and I'm taking you out on the town tonight!" He pulled off her apron and pushed her in the direction of the stairs, without pausing for any response. "I'll call Mom and tell her I'm bringing the kids over in ten minutes to stay overnight."

"They have school tomorrow."

Kurt's smile was dazzling as he wiggled his eyebrows. "I'll talk to her really sweetly and ask her to take them to school in the morning. Don't worry . . . be happy! Go get ready."

Polly shook her head as she headed up to their bedroom. A million details swam around her tired brain. *Tommy's social studies project is due* tomorrow. *Amy has a piano lesson tonight—I guess I'll have to call and cancel that. Anna needs to take her viola to school tomorrow for lessons. The baby . . .* "Aghhh!" She pivoted toward the baby's room and began gathering articles into the larger of the two diaper bags. *I can't do this. This is crazy. I should just have told him no. Maybe tomorrow night.* She threw two extra sets of onesies into the bag for good measure. *Stop. Take a deep breath. Is this possible? Never mind. What's next?*

Kurt's voice boomed on the floor below as he jollied the kids into collecting their stuff for the trip to their grandmother's. "Come on. Let's go. We don't want to keep Gramma waitin.' Let's go, let's go!"

Upstairs, Polly shook her head as she grabbed the bags and hustled Tommy downstairs with them. *Maybe I should tell him this is crazy.*

"Hello there, sweetheart!" Kurt stood at the bottom of the stairs, beaming up at her.

I love to see him like this. Polly couldn't resist smiling back. *I can't tell him this is impossible.* "When are we leaving?"

"As soon as I get back from Mom's—maybe fifteen minutes." He was already herding the kids out to the car with the baby carrier under one arm. "Back soon, beautiful."

Polly raced into their bedroom, mentally checking jobs off the list. Grabbing the phone, she punched in the piano teacher's number and looked up to see her untidy reflection in the bedroom mirror. She gasped. *I can't possibly be ready in fifteen minutes . . . not even half an hour. Oh, I should have told him no! We haven't been out like this in months. Why does it have to be so sudden? We miss all the anticipation.* She sighed, as a little voice in her head said, "You should have spoken up sooner."

Polly has a problem speaking, period. She thinks a lot, but she doesn't verbalize her thoughts. People can only guess what she's thinking. And most of the time, they guess wrong. Polly always looks pleasant, demonstrates polite and appropriate actions, and seems happy. Oh, if only they knew. If only Kurt knew—he'd be very surprised.

189

"I am so disgusted with you!" Wendy stood in the doorway to the family room and addressed Ted slouched in his chair by the TV.

He flipped off the TV and frowned at Wendy.

"Can you not see what needs to be done around here *before* we can *both* relax and enjoy the evening?" She gestured at newspapers littering the floor, a few soda cans, and an empty ice-cream carton and then waved toward the kitchen. "Or do you just expect me to do *everything* around the house *and* work a full-time job?"

She turned her back on him, while slinging words over her shoulder in his general direction. "This kitchen floor needs to be mopped, and I don't know anyone with your muscular physique who can't push a mop around a floor. It escapes me how you can be so lazy and self-consumed."

Ted followed her into the kitchen, only to have a mop handle shoved into his hand.

"I just don't get it. Before we got married, you told me you liked to cook." Wendy shrugged her shoulders and put her hands on her elegant hips. "You haven't cooked more than a meal here or there for the past year. Tonight's your night." She picked up her briefcase and glared at Ted. "I'm going to change. Get busy, buster."

Wendy has no inhibitions about speaking the truth. Problem—presentation! There is little respect, love, or compassion expressed, and no thought regarding what Ted is experiencing as she flings the truth at him.

THE WAY WE SPEAK

Not all people are created equal when it comes to speaking. Some speak a lot, some not very much. Some folks are soft-spoken, and others are outspoken. Some people are wordy, while others are concise and to the point. Some speak with authority; others end every sentence with the uptilt of a question, as if they are not sure of the thought they've spoken.

I tend to speak almost every thought. I think out loud. On the other hand, Rich processes his thoughts internally and generally speaks only proven theories and facts. Given Rich's way of thinking/speaking, he tends to take my every word as truth when, in fact, it is often mere suggestion. When he becomes disappointed with me, he claims I lied. On the other hand, I don't always take him seriously, thinking he is brain-storming ideas as I like to do. Later, I find out he was serious about what he said, and I'm in trouble again!

The ways Rich and I think, speak, and react come from our person-alities: He's the aggressive, mover-shaker choleric, and I'm the people-party-person, happy-go-lucky sanguine. We were also influenced by our birth culture: He was born in the Bronx of New York City and raised on Long Island, and I grew up in Lancaster County, Pennsylvania, where Amish and Mennonite pacifism is a way of life. It's easy to see why I tend to be the effervescent peacemaker and Rich is the curt commander.

Can you relate to Meghan, Polly, or Wendy, or to me or Rich? Are you one who speaks too little . . . or too much? Do you speak the unpol-ished, candid truth? Or are you too afraid to voice what might hurt someone else's feelings? Do you say what people want to hear . . . or what they need to hear?

What is your communication style? Are you truthful? How truthful? Do you speak "the truth, the whole truth, and nothing but the truth"? Do you *speak with sincerity?*

Listen to the words of the apostle Paul to the church at Ephesus: "*Speaking the truth in love,* we will in all things grow up into him who is the Head, that is, Christ. From him the whole body, joined and held together by every supporting ligament, grows and builds itself up in love, as each part does its work" (Ephesians 4:15–16, italics added).

Jesus is our best example of *speaking the truth in love.* In the book of John, Jesus is described: "The Word became flesh and made his dwelling among us. We have seen his glory, the glory of the One and Only, who came from the Father, *full of grace and truth*" (John 1:14, italics added). The late pastor Ralph Stoll pointed out that "Jesus was not so gracious that He wasn't truthful, and not so truthful that He wasn't gracious." Oh, that people would have reason to describe us in such a way!

Grace and truth may appear to be opposite extremes. Grace is loving and giving—the more-than-you-deserve attribute that flows from com-passion. On the other hand, truth can be cold, hard, and unyielding. Truth is truth. In a court of law, on the basis of truth as the court sees it, you are tried, convicted, and sentenced. Where is God on these two opposing issues? Is He not both gracious and truthful? Can we be both? Alas, we tend to gravitate toward one end or the other.

In *Speaking the Truth in Love: How to Be an Assertive Christian*, Ruth N. Kock and Kenneth C. Haugk define the middle ground as "assertiveness."

Aggressive	Assertive	Passive
(truth without grace)		(grace without truth)

Assertiveness is the balance between being aggressive and being passive. An assertive Christian is one who speaks the truth graciously—both elements are present. To be assertive Christians, Meghan and Polly must learn to *speak the truth,* and Wendy needs to speak the truth *in love.*

> By behaving assertively, people begin to see themselves, as well as others, as individuals who are important and who have feelings, ideas, opinions, and rights that are worthy of expression. Assertive behavior can mean expressing all those aspects of self without resorting to threats, hostility, manipulation, or other aggressive actions. And it can mean experiencing those expressions from others without considering oneself threatened, abused, intimidated, or victimized.[1]

Jesus, our perfect example of assertiveness, acted and spoke the truth in love. As a perfectly assertive person, He sometimes chose, based on the situation, to be aggressive or passive. For example, He angrily threw the moneychangers out of His Father's temple. On the other hand, He reacted passively to the people who abused and mistreated Him in the last days of His life on earth. Even as Jesus acted appropriately in each situation, so we can rely on God to help us respond properly to circumstances and people in our lives.

Can a naturally aggressive, take-charge woman become assertive? Can a timid, quiet wife learn to function assertively before an overbearing husband? Yes, we can learn to *speak the truth in love.*

Going back to the line showing aggression at one end and pacifism at the other, where are you?

Let's examine the two key elements of godly speaking: speaking the truth, and speaking in love. *Speaking the truth in love* reflects God's character. The concept of *assertive Christianity* helps us speak the necessary candid truth with a consistent attitude of complete love and acceptance for the other person (for the person, *not necessarily his behavior*).

Speaking the *Truth*

Our young people are being taught there is no such thing as absolute truth. Without absolute truth, where is a foundation for my life or yours? Does this not make every person an authority unto himself? I don't mind telling you that the idea of being unable to know truth scares me.

Second Timothy 1:7 says, "For God did not give us a spirit of timidity, but a spirit of power, of love and of self-discipline." Put the fear away. God's answer is self-discipline, or the KJV's "sound mind"—knowing that we live by a very definite set of laws and standards, set up for our benefit by the God who loves us and wants the best for us. As we obediently live within His protective and enabling framework, we grow and mature in every way to be more like Him. When we disobey and live outside His loving boundaries, our hearts and minds become more and more calloused and far from God and truth. The truth in God's Word, the Bible, must be our standard for living. This truth gives us power for living, compassionate love for the people around us, and minds that we can discipline to think on the things of God.

The final, absolute truth is God Himself. In John 14:6, Jesus says, "I am the way and the *truth* and the life." If God is truth, anything contrary to truth is in opposition to His very being. Falsehood, dishonesty, deceit, and little white lies cannot be tolerated by one who is, Himself, truth.

The first lie was told in the garden to Eve, by the Father of Lies, Satan (John 8:44). God said to Adam and Eve, "For when you eat of it [the Tree of the Knowledge of Good and Evil] you will surely die" (Genesis 2:17). But the serpent, which "was more crafty than any of the wild animals the LORD God had made," came along and said to Eve, "You will not surely die! . . . For God knows that when you eat of it your eyes will be opened, and you will be like God, knowing good and evil" (Genesis 3:1, 4–5). The rest is history.

Through people, situations, and even our own thinking, Satan lies to us. This crafty devil does not tell us outright, obvious lies. More often his lies take the form of exaggeration and distortion of the truth—mutilated and stretched out of proportion until we cannot see reality clearly. We function, then, in a surreal existence, a fantasy—good or bad—of our own making when we are blinded to the truth and the God of truth.

On the flip side of the coin, we ourselves have become liars. When we live in a world of untruths, we find it easy to dissimulate. We fudge a little on our taxes. We tell ourselves it's OK to go five or ten miles over the speed limit because we're a traffic hazard if we don't keep up with the other cars, and then we go the ten-miles-over when there's no other traffic around. We exaggerate to make a story more captivating. We create "logical explanations" that don't include all of the facts in order to get "off the hook." We lie to get revenge, to make a profit, for convenience, to impress, and to escape punishment. And we become good at it. Everyone does it, we rationalize. Everyone but God.

If three people witness an automobile accident from three different corners of an intersection, do they all tell the same story? No, each person recounts what his own eyes saw from his personal perspective. If God were recalling the accident, the account would be perfect, for He sees from every dimension—many which we have yet to understand.

Therefore, my personal truth is not God's perfect truth, but merely my own limited understanding and application of truthful principles. Because I am finite, I can continue to learn, grasp, and understand components of truth, but I must depend on the Holy Spirit daily to live according to God's will for my life and the world.

How does the truth set a wife free from an angry, selfish husband? The truth liberates us above circumstances. Blame, shame, and abuse don't stick if you don't let them! When I know Rich is seeing something from only his perspective and is expecting too much of me, I ask God for the *truth* and then refuse to accept Rich's accusations or disapproval. I remind myself that, although Rich sees this as my problem, the real problem is his heart being closed to the Holy Spirit who leads, resulting in poor perspective. Any one of us at any time can become self-indulgently critical, nitpicky, or grumpy about something we perceive someone has done to upset our personal world. (We'll talk more about dealing honestly with a difficult husband in the next chapter.)

The first aspect of godly communication is speaking the truth. To speak the truth, we must desire to know it, and we must intentionally set our minds on it. When truth reigns, we can confess sin, find forgiveness and grace, and solve problems. When we live with lies, half-truths, and deception, the world is unsteady. We selfishly look out for our own interests, missing God's solutions to our problems, with the result of becoming defeated, discouraged, and desolate. Truth is liberating.

But truth alone is not enough. The truth, alone, can sometimes hurt. Truth can be ugly, hurtful, and cold. God calls us to temper it with grace, which is a by-product of love.

Speaking in *Love*

Love is so much more than "warm fuzzies." The love we are talking about is not just an emotion, but an attitude that produces action. An attitude of respect and compassion plays out in every aspect of godly communication.

The attitude of unselfish humility is defined in Philippians 2. Verses 3 and 4 say: "Do nothing out of selfish ambition or vain conceit, but in humility consider others better than yourselves. Each of you should look not only to your own interests, but also to the interests of others." This is a decision to not focus on me, my, and mine, but on the other person. Verse 5 starts, "Your attitude should be the same as that of Christ Jesus." Just like the "What Would Jesus Do?" slogan, this verse asks us to *think* about the truth, and then speak or act on it from a loving, others-centered perspective. *Thinking first* is a real challenge for many of us—but commanded and beneficial nevertheless. Verse 14 reminds us, "Do everything without complaining or arguing."

It is easy to be loving when life runs smoothly. But, as "Murphy's Laws" for marriage point out, life is rarely predictable:

• No matter which two people marry, one inevitably squeezes the toothpaste tube from the end and the other from the middle.

- A person who likes to be coddled when sick marries someone who crawls under a rock when ill and thinks everyone else should too.
- Only when there are dishes in the sink, clothes in the dryer waiting to be folded, bathrooms needing to be cleaned, and you're not feeling well, will your spouse suggest going out to dinner and a movie.
- One turns up the heat while the other opens the windows.
- Your husband's worst day at work will invariably coincide with your first day of PMS—during which the kids can't get along, the car is making odd clunking sounds, and the cat is gakking up hairballs on the carpet.
- No matter how wonderful your mate is, your friend's husband will have a totally enviable quality your husband doesn't—and possess none of the annoying traits belonging to your husband.
- A husband who can't find his socks always seems to know the location of the television remote control.
- Husbands who run successful businesses with multiple employees panic when left in charge of the kids for an afternoon.

Humore aside, even when two people make the most of their marriage, the road of life is filled with unexpected bumps. Successful living takes the knowledge of God's truth—who He is, what He is doing, how His work is affecting our lives, and His love for us.

The world offers no such truth or love. God *is* our guarantee, as He was for the psalmist David, who said,

> *Do not withhold your mercy from me, O LORD; may **your love and your truth** always protect me. For troubles without number surround me; my sins have overtaken me, and I cannot see. They are more than the hairs of my head, and my heart fails within me. Be pleased, O LORD, to save me; O LORD, come quickly to help me. (Psalm 40:11–13, emphasis added)*

In this dangerous and unfair world, God gives us absolute truth as the basis for living out the unique lives He has created for each one of us. His unconditional love keeps us going in all circumstances, for we know that nothing can separate us from His love. Furthermore, His love begets our love—not the heady, emotional feeling of earthly bliss, but a real compassion for others that demonstrates itself in everyday actions, attitudes, and words—*spoken in love.*

A Closing Application

Perhaps the best example of *speaking the truth in love* came from a friend whom I will call Mike. He and his wife traveled, along with her father, back to a church Mike had planted and pastored several years before. Church growth had brought about the need for a new building, and Mike and his family took a short vacation in order to help with the construction.

On the top of the hot roof, nailing shingles, Mike missed a stroke and drove a nail right through his finger. Fortunately one of the men on the site was an EMT, with a bag of medical supplies close by. Soon Mike's finger was properly medicated and bandaged, and he stubbornly climbed back up the roof to resume his task, albeit awkwardly.

Working nearby was his father-in-law, known to say whatever he was thinking, usually when it shouldn't be said. After several minutes, within everyone's hearing, he asked Mike, "So what's the next stupid thing you're gonna do?"

Silence filled the air, as his former parishioners awaited Mike's reply. Praying for the right words, he answered with a question of his own, delivered with a slight chuckle. "Just what part of that remark is supposed to be helpful?" Great answer! The truth said, "Your remark was unnecessary." Grace softened the truth by freeing Mike's comment from blame, anger, and insult by adding a gentle chuckle. He asked a question that was honest, and caused his father-in-law to face his error, without shaming him for his critical comment.

Mike held his ground. He didn't play the pacifist and allow himself to be belittled. Neither did he aggressively fight back and play one-upmanship. He assertively stood toe-to-toe with his father-in-law and stated the truth in love.

Do you hesitate when you know you could say something? Are you the one who blames, the one who must be "king of the mountain"? Or are you God's assertive child, holding on to the truth, and sharing it with love, grace, and compassion?

Go and *speak the truth in love!*

> *Dear Jesus,*
> *Teach me to be like You: full of grace and truth. Help me to as-*
> *sertively speak the truth—with a gracious delivery from a truly*
> *loving heart.*

18

Stand Your Ground

*W*illard F. Harley Jr., author of *Give and Take: The Secret of Marital Compatibility,* identifies "givers" and "takers" in the marriage relationship. He defines the rules of the giver and the taker as follows: "The Giver's Rule: Do whatever you can to make the other person happy and avoid anything that makes the other person unhappy. The Taker's Rule: Do whatever you can to make yourself happy and avoid anything that makes you unhappy."[1]

To restore balance, harmony, and intimacy in the marriage relationship, Harley suggests a policy of joint agreement: "Never do anything without an enthusiastic agreement between you and your spouse."[2] This is great, when you actually have two parties who agree. But women (and men) are in lopsided marriages. *Give and Take* can be an excellent tool for *couples* who desire a closer relationship.

But what does a wife do, by herself, in a marriage where her spouse isn't cooperative?

If you are the "giver" in your marriage, and all you ever seem to "take" is a lot of mild abuse, this chapter is for you. Let me restate that if you are experiencing abuse that puts you in physical, mental, or emotional *danger,* you need to get immediate help—call a friend, pastor, or Christian counselor now! However, if you are tired of dealing with a husband who is aggressive and dominant by nature (natural personality bents and/or sin nature), I hope this chapter will encourage your heart and teach you how to stand in the midst of the storm.

In truth, we have no direct control over the actions of another person. But how we react to others' actions is within our grasp. We can learn to re-act appropriately to every kind of outside stimulus. How do you generally take what's handed, shoved, or hurled at you? And *what do you do with it?*

In the last chapter, Meghan and Polly *passively* reacted to negative situations: backing off, trying to smooth over, and ignoring problems. These ineffective actions did not ease their situations. On the other hand, Wendy quite *aggressively* placed demands on Ted. Her "I'm right and I will win" attitude did little to inspire or motivate Ted.

Kock and Haugk, in *Speaking the Truth in Love,* tell us more about godly assertive behavior:

> *Assertive behavior is behavior that honors the self while honoring others. The assertive person authentically cares for others and at the same time engages in God-pleasing self-care.*
>
> *Assertive behavior is a constructive way of living and relating to other people. It is behavior that reflects concern about being honest, direct, open, and natural in relations with others.*
>
> *Assertiveness encompasses a wide variety of actions. For example, assertive behavior may involve standing up for your rights. It may involve genuinely expressing your affection-ate feelings to another person. Assertive behavior may mean giving as well as receiving compliments. And it might involve saying yes to some requests and saying no to other requests.*
>
> *Individuals who think and behave assertively are people who have an active orientation to life, people who participate fully in life, people with a sense of God-given personal power. Assertive men and women live decisively, aware that life is full of choices and sensitive to their responsibility to make decisions about those choices.*[3]

Kock and Haugk give these attitudes and behaviors of assertiveness:

- Assertive Christians believe they have options.
- Assertive Christians are proactive.
- Assertive Christians believe God values each person.
- Assertive Christians are motivated by love.
- Assertive Christians stand up for themselves without excessive anxiety.
- Assertive Christians are people of integrity.
- Assertive Christians accept their own limitations and the limitations of others.
- Assertive Christians practice self-revelation within appropriate personal boundaries.
- Assertive Christians can choose to behave assertively, aggressively, or passively.
- Assertive Christians believe that every person has certain basic human rights.[4]

There are times in every marriage when a wife needs to confront, correct, or communicate negative information to her husband, or simply react in a difficult situation.

My husband stands well over six feet tall and possesses a strong choleric/melancholy personality. Rich can be frightfully intimidating. When he finds fault with me, my natural reaction is to run and hide, or at least cower and try to fix the situation (in his favor) as quickly as possible. Why do I "give in"? Because I feel intimidated. And I don't like to feel small and stupid, so I selfishly try to resolve the situation that is making him unhappy, which will ultimately take the heat off me. I passively yield under the pressure of the moment.

After I've allowed myself to be overwhelmed and belittled, I selfishly want to retaliate. So, to my shame, I turn into the aggressor with Becky, our daughter. She's smaller and more easily controlled. When I have a need for power after feeling oppressed by Rich's intimidation (even if it was my problem to begin with), I have a sinful tendency to lash out at Becky for anything she has done wrong. I can't tell you how many times

I've realized what I'm doing and wanted to run away and hide. How can such a loving mother be so miserable toward her own child?

Examine who was at fault in both of the above scenarios. Me? Rich? Becky? Let's ask the question in a different way. Did I do something wrong that upset Rich? Let's say I did. Did he handle his frustration with grace and compassion? No. Had Becky done something wrong that needed to be corrected? Probably, somewhere along the line. But, did I correct her graciously, with loving compassion? No. Each of us was wrong.

CHOOSING NOT TO BE REACTIVE

Are you reactive? Our reactions are often a truer test of who we are than our actions are.

Jesus taught His disciples, "The good man brings good things out of the good stored up in his heart, and the evil man brings evil things out of the evil stored up in his heart. For out of the overflow of his heart his mouth speaks" (Luke 6:45). What fills my heart will spill over into my life and out on the people around me. Jesus is more concerned about my heart motives than my good manners. He is more interested in my attitudes than my actions.

Most of life is not action, but reaction to life around us. I generally respond or react according to my emotions, not my rational mind. My feelings are fed data by sensory preceptors: what my eyes see, the texture touched by my fingertips, etc. However, my emotions are reactive, not rational. Emotions may be first to accurately recognize something is wrong, but they can't be counted on to suggest the best way to respond. If I employ my mind to think through the issue, I will be able to respond more appropriately than if I get carried away with the emotion of the moment. Reacting to the emotions without stopping to think and analyze can be dangerous.

CHOOSING TO BE PROACTIVE

Proactive behavior takes steps to avoid problems before they occur, thus reducing the need for *reaction*. How does this work in marriage? How does this relate to becoming an assertive Christian?

I must learn to act and react in the way God intends. To be proactive, I must start with my attitude. I must desire above all else to be the person God wants me to be and "go for it" regardless of the situation.

In *Strengthening Your Grip*, Chuck Swindoll relates the story of Nicolo Paganini, an accomplished violinist, whose violin strings began breaking during a concert. As he completed the final number with only one string, the Italian audience jumped to its feet, cheering and applauding. As he hushed them, he nodded to the conductor to begin the encore and shouted to the audience, "Paganini . . . and one string." He did it. Amazing!

Swindoll says,

Words can never adequately convey the incredible impact of our attitude toward life. The longer I live the more convinced I become that life is 10 percent what happens to us and 90 percent how we respond to it. This may shock you, but I believe the single most significant decision I can make on a day-to-day basis is my choice of attitude. It is more important than my past, my education, my bankroll, my successes or failures, fame or pain, what other people think of me or say about me, my circumstances, or my position. Attitude is that "single string" that keeps me going or cripples my progress. It alone fuels my fire or assaults my hope. When my attitudes are right, there's no barrier too high, no valley too deep, no dream too extreme, no challenge too great for me. [5]

This requires maturity.

So how do I *proactively* learn to behave as God intends? Although directly related to my feelings, the answer is in my mind. I control myself through my mind, not my feelings. However, it is natural to react based on feelings, rather than purely on truth. The truth can seem unclear in my mind when it is dulled by the intense feelings I am experiencing.

During a severe struggle with myself, based on this issue of the mind, I found help through a counselor who taught me about the abuser-victim-rescuer triangle. I began to identify myself as an abuser (with Becky), a victim (with Rich), and sometimes even a rescuer (when I think Rich is being hard on Becky). I learned if I refuse to play one of the parts, the triangle falls apart—without one of the three corners, a triangle is not a triangle. If I make the choice not to act like a victim, there can be no triangle—no abuse—no fight. The answer is in my mind, and in my will to choose.

This reasoning will not work in a truly abusive marriage where the wife needs to seek professional help. However, in a "normal" marriage to a difficult person, you can choose *not* to be a victim.

I do a bit of self-talk, when faced with a husband who is acting domineering or unfair. I remind myself that he is not seeing the truth as I see it. I ask God to help me see His truth clearly. Instant gratification wants me to react emotionally, but I choose to allow God to speak truth to my mind and pour His love for Rich into my heart. I also trust Him to give me wisdom to speak truth when the time is right.

The bottom line is: I don't have to be a victim if I don't choose to be one. "Well, Nancy," you say, "why would anyone want to be a victim?" There is certain appeal in playing the victim. Haven't you ever thought, *I deserve to feel terrible—if this happened to anyone else, they'd feel miserable too!* We have this penchant for "the pit." We even take others with us—we call them up and invite them to our "pit-y party!" Remember this old chant?

Nobody loves me, everybody hates me,

I'm going to go eat worms.

The two extremes of action/reaction are blame and self-pity. The aggressive person blames everyone but herself. The passive person pities herself, crawls into a hole (the pit), and licks her wounds. I am proactive when I choose *not* to be a victim, *not* to be passive, but to see and declare God's truth in this situation. I am proactive when I choose to be an assertive, balanced Christian with a positive attitude.

IF YOUR HUSBAND IS AGGRESSIVE

Just how can you communicate assertively with someone who challenges, accuses, or threatens you aggressively and unfairly? What do you do with an argumentative accuser? In short, how do you deal with a difficult spouse?

Dr. Joyce Hulgus, a dear friend and astoundingly wise professional psychologist, stayed in our home for several months during her move from the West Coast back to the East. One of her signature quotes I've come to greatly appreciate is "Truth Resonates." The principle is as simple as it sounds. When you speak the truth—simply and directly, with no emotion to cloud the issue—the truth will bounce around and echo in the other person's heart, mind, and life. And *truth cannot be denied.* This resonating process sometimes takes what seems like an eternity, but the truth always remains. In this life, truth can be ignored or justified away, but in the end God's truth will stand.

In applying this principle, especially when dealing with an angry, adamant person, Joyce recommends that the truth-speaker be "lean and brief." For "lean," picture a steak with little fat—all meat. "Brief" means short and to the point.

The truth-speaker's content is as important as her delivery. First, she must clearly identify the other person's problem *pattern.* As an example, Polly observes Kurt keeping up a crazy pace of exciting, spontaneous activity around the house, without allowing less energetic people, like Polly and the kids, to enjoy any relaxing "down time." Polly has identified a repeating problem in Kurt's home life, as it relates to her and their children. Unemotionally, cognitively (using her mind), she must figure out the healing truth that corresponds with the problem. What change is necessary in Kurt's behavior, for his sake and his family's, and how can that be realized?

At this point, it is very necessary for Polly to pray for strength, boldness, and godly compassion for her husband. She is doing what is right for herself, her husband, and their family. Praying and listening to prompts from the Holy Spirit, she waits for the right time and place to speak the truth in love.

In the ten minutes before Kurt must leave to pick up a take-out pizza order for supper, Polly asks him to step out to the garage with her for a short talk. As they lean against the cars, she quickly, calmly, and with a few choice words explains the problem she has seen and what could be done to resolve it. "Kurt, I need to honestly tell you that the kids and I need more quiet family time. I know you love to be out and about, and I commend you for your incredible stamina and energy level. However, watching and praying for you, I believe you have a problem being too involved with activities. At home, we need you to sit quietly with us from time to time, and listen. May I be so bold as to suggest you need some down time with yourself and God, too? Because I love you, I wanted to share this with you and tell you I'm here if I can be of help to you in any way." (This approach is far superior to hurtful words thrown out in the anger of the moment, or cold silence distancing them from each other.)

If the truth-speaker's communication toward the difficult person presents *lean and brief* truth, she has said as much as is required in that moment. Now it's time to back off, live the truth she has proclaimed, and wait until "truth resonates." Fullness comes in the living out of truth. It is critical *not* to withdraw or pout, but to remain present in the relationship —solid and loving.

Rich's general speech epitomizes "lean and brief," because he has a choleric personality—direct, realistic, and to the point. This type of person gets to the bottom line quickly and in a hurry. The other personalities experience more difficulty with this concept. Sanguines just plain talk too much under pressure. They will say the same thing a million different ways, hoping to get the point across and all of the details "out on the table." Melancholies are afraid of saying the wrong thing and getting into trouble. So, when they speak, they generally come across as negative and critical. They're actually nervous about making sure they say the right thing. The phlegmatic-type person, with a dry wit, will possibly resort to sarcasm and mumbling—if he is forced to say anything at all. Most times, phlegmatics close their eyes (and mouths) and hope the whole thing blows over quickly.

Through teaching, loving, and listening to hurting wives over the past several years, I've noticed one thing we all have in common. We're not sure what we have a right to expect, how much to ask for, and what is fair to desire from our spouses. Do we really have any rights as women, or did we give them up when we accepted Christ as Savior and signed on to be His ambassadors?

I'm indebted to Kock and Haugk, who put into writing the following list of "basic human rights." The first time I read this list, I felt a tremendous freedom in my spirit as my mind grasped these truths. The list includes:

- Each person has the right to be treated respectfully.
- Each person has the right to say no without explanation and without guilt.

- Each person has the right to slow down and take time to think.
- Each person has the right to change his or her mind.
- Each person has the right to ask for what he or she wants.
- Each person has the right to ask for information.
- Each person has the right to make mistakes.
- Each person has the right to make choices and accept the consequences of those choices.
- Each person has the right to own and express his or her own feelings.
- Each person has the right to ask for help.
- Each person has the right to maintain a separate self that is accountable to God and independent of the expectations, the approval, or the influence of others.[6]

I must respect these rights in other people's lives as I relate to each person. And this is how I can ask others to treat me. Note I did not say this is how I can *expect* others to treat me. I must *stand* on my own two feet and, by the power and grace of God, declare my right and need for these considerations in my own life.

God's command in Ephesians is this:

> *Finally, be strong in the Lord and in his mighty power. Put on the full armor of God so that you can take your **stand** against the devil's schemes. . . . Therefore put on the full armor of God, so that when the day of evil comes, you may be able to **stand** your ground, and after you have done everything, to **stand**. **Stand** firm then, with the **belt of truth** buckled around your waist. (Ephesians 6:10–11, 13–14, emphasis added)*

A first-century Roman soldier's wide leather belt was the foundational piece of his entire uniform (and Rome outfitted her army far better than any other nation—thus their successes). All loose articles of clothing —the tunic and so on—were connected to the body by the belt. Thus the belt held the soldier together. Furthermore, onto the belt were attached all the articles of combat and defense. Without the belt, a soldier was not equipped. The belt in Paul's analogy very accurately corresponds to the truth in the believer's life. Without God's truth, we fall apart and are ill equipped for the battles we face.

Though we live in the world, we do not wage war as the world does. The weapons we fight with are not the weapons of the world. On the contrary, they have divine power to demolish strongholds. We demolish arguments and every pretension that sets itself up against the knowledge of God, and we take captive every thought to make it obedient to Christ.
(2 Corinthians 10:3–5)

Are you clothed with God's truth, standing firm in the battle?

By placing your faith in God and obeying His precepts, will all your problems with your husband and your marriage be erased? Sadly, the answer is no. In a fallen world, not every relationship has a happy ending. Does that always mean we didn't stand tall enough, practice the truth soundly enough, praise God joyfully enough? No. Some women have married incorrigible men—men who have no intention of giving up their search for self-satisfaction, ever. (And some men have married egotistical women.)

However, hope remains. It just has different faces. God sometimes allows a difficult phase of life to come to an end—and in the next phase, hope takes on a different face. Even in the life of Christ, whom religious leaders trapped, humiliated, and murdered, His end brought a new beginning. "And God is faithful; he will not let you be tempted beyond what you can bear. But when you are tempted, he will also provide a way out so that you can stand up under it" (1 Corinthians 10:13). Stand tall, sister in Christ.

Can you live an assertive, positive, healthy life in a household with an argumentative, aggressive, self-centered spouse? Yes, and you can teach your children how to become assertive, mature individuals who speak the truth in love. This is a tough topic to master, but it can be done with God's grace and His Spirit. Sometimes God grants us helpers "with skin on" to come alongside us in times of trouble. Don't be afraid to ask for help.

> *O God of Truth,*
> *Help me know and live Your truth. Please give me a discerning*
> *mind and heart, and boldness to declare the truth at the right time*
> *and in the right way.*

Intimacy Renewed

Dear God,
You've brought me so far already that I
choose to bring You into our bedroom.
I need You to shape my thoughts
and feelings about intimacy.
Make me the wife I need to be
for Your glory and our joy.

19

Rekindle the Romance

*A*ngie slid under the covers, trying not to disturb her sleeping husband. Facing away from Nick, on the very edge of the bed, relief surged through her body when she heard his deep breathing resume. She stared at the luminous numbers on the clock. *I'm not sleepy now, but I'll be exhausted tomorrow morning.* Her mind rehearsed the events of the past day. Nick had verbally sparred with her in front of the kids. She remembered every word he'd said. Tears puddled in the corners of her eyes and trickled toward the pillow.

Lord, how do You expect me to love this man, when he can be so mean at times? I'm at the point where I can't even stand the thought of being touched. This is my husband, Lord. I'm not supposed to feel this way. Help me! Angie wiped more tears away, and Nick rolled toward her in his sleep. Reaching his arm around her, he pulled her toward him.

Lord, please don't let him wake up. I'm just not in the mood for sex tonight. Angie willed her body to relax. *This isn't how it's supposed to be! I want to be a good wife, but how can I be loving in bed when he is so unloving everywhere else?* Angie wondered how long it had been since she'd last felt "in love" with Nick, and she questioned what she could do to bring back that loving feeling.

More than seven or eight years ago, I could have been Angie in this scene. I was tired of being misunderstood, disrespected, and put down. I had allowed Rich's cruel words and frustrating behavior to send me to an all-time low of 0 percent human love. The fun "tingles" had disappeared early in our marriage. Excitement had gradually been replaced by routines. And the mystery of sexual love had been dissipated by the old adage "familiarity breeds contempt." Worst of all, the love I promised Rich at our wedding became difficult to live up to as the years went by. With each change of schedule, job, and lifestyle, my natural love for Rich weakened. What was left totally evaporated with his second back surgery, his recuperation, and his resulting anger. We were merely roommates.

At the lowest point in our marriage, I had zero interest in the physical side of love. Lucky for me, Rich's health problems coincided with most of that period of time, so I didn't need to deflect romantic overtures very often. But all the joy was gone. I didn't even like him very much, let alone love him. During that time, I began searching for something I could do to make this marriage relationship work—at least from my side. Slowly, through mentoring relationships, counseling, good books, and a deepening relationship with God, He brought back peace, joy, and fun. And, finally, "the tingles" returned! I'm living proof—you *can* fall in love all over again.

Before we look at the "how" of falling in love again, we need to look at the reality of life. Life isn't always fair, nor is it always perfect. Even though God is able to restore relationships, sometimes He chooses to allow unresolved difficulty in our lives in order to bring glory to His name in ways beyond our understanding. Physical love may be an area in your life that is just impossible at this time for one of many reasons. A woman who is physically unable to enjoy the romantic aspects of a loving relationship may have to settle for less than she desires. Another woman might find it difficult to reconcile physically to a husband who has been unfaithful, even though she has taken him back into their home. God is always good, but He does not solve all of our problems all of the time. If you are finding this topic a bit overwhelming, try taking a moment to talk to God about it and ask Him to read with you—or even skip from here to the conclusion. (Come back when you are ready.)

How can you bring back that loving feeling? How do you learn to be "in love" again? In various parts of the Bible, most notably the Song of Songs, God encourages us to desire intimacy with our spouse. But what if the passion has fizzled?

OUT OF LOVE

Dr. Douglas E. Rosenau has encouraging words for the disenchanted wife:

> *Do you want to be in love? If you do, you can. The reasons that got you married are seldom all the ones that keep you married. If you desire, today can be the beginning of your new marriage. God has given you a marvelous capacity in your rational mind to think and make choices. You can mobilize your will and choose to follow through on behaviors that will create loving feelings. You can rework your past attitudes and learning. Attitudes and behaviors are the bases of feeling in love and not some mysterious chemistry of feelings that you cannot control.*[1]

I became excited when I first read these words, because they accurately described what was happening in my life as I chose to love Rich and act out that decision and commitment. Go back and read the quote again. Notice the tools God has given you to make love happen: a rational mind and a will to choose. The initial decision to love again is followed by the hard work of appropriate actions and attitudes.

Contemplate the "arranged marriage" still in use in many Eastern countries. If two strangers can build a loving relationship, certainly love can be reclaimed and rebuilt.

Just like a house that has become run-down and needs renovation, so a couple's love life may need to be reconstructed—possibly from the ground up. The foundation of a strong love relationship is a clear understanding of (1) what God designed, (2) how we humans tend to mess up God's plan, and (3) why we have trouble with this topic. With a solid foundation in place, we then build up a workable *framework* of actions and attitudes that hold strong amidst raging storms and bad weather. Finally, feelings of love will become the *decorations* that make the house a home—they are the easy, fun part of the building process, but generally the last step.

STOP! What if I'm at the point where I don't even have the desire to try to love my husband again? Before you read any farther, take some time to stop and pray. Then, call your prayer partner or a close friend who will pray and hold you accountable. Ask this person to pray (1) for you to *see and believe God's truth about love and sex*, (2) for you to *know and obey what God commands*, and (3) for God to *give you a renewed love for your husband, small step by small step*. Then continue reading, with a heart and mind open to the Holy Spirit's teaching.

THE FOUNDATION OF A LOVING RELATIONSHIP

Unfortunately, many people believe love, romance, and sex are optional, not integral parts of a marriage. Even if they don't start out with this notion, tyranny of the urgent often pushes the fun parts of love into the background. What priority do *you* place on the romantic aspect of your marriage? What comes before fun with your mate?

Why Did God Create This Aspect of Marriage?

God puts a high priority on physical love in marriage. Scripture gives us several reasons.

1. Sex is re-creational. Genesis 1:28 expounds on sex for the purpose of reproduction. "God blessed [Adam and Eve] and said to them, 'Be fruitful and increase in number; fill the earth.'" Although cloning animals and body parts may lead us to believe we can replicate living things, only God gives life. Sex was His original creation, designed to reproduce generations of people with whom He could relate.

2. Married sex promotes unity and knowledge between husband and wife. "A man will leave his father and mother and be united to his wife." God further describes that relationship by saying, "They will become one flesh" (Genesis 2:24). One flesh is the joining of the male and female bodies—two parts of a whole. I like the King James wording for that joining: "Adam *knew* Eve his wife" (Genesis 4:1, italics added). No one knows you better than the one who sleeps with you and makes love to your body. Another expression for sex is "being intimate," and surely no one knows me more intimately than the man who literally sees me "in the flesh."

3. Proverbs 5:19 suggests both intimacy and pleasure should be parts of sex. "A loving doe, a graceful deer—may her breasts satisfy you always, may you ever be captivated by her love." Surely romance and sex were created to provide exquisite pleasure. The Song of Songs is filled with expressions of pleasure, desire, and passion. This book is included in God's Word as a testimony to the importance God places on sex and loving desire.

4. A satisfying physical relationship with a spouse also protects against temptation. Hebrews 13:4 says "Marriage should be honored by all, and the marriage bed kept pure, for God will judge the adulterer and all the sexually immoral." You can keep *yourself* pure from adultery, pornography, and other forms of sexual sins, but can you do anything to help your husband stay pure and true to you? Although you are not responsible for fulfilling inappropriate or ungodly desires, there are many things you can do to keep him in your bed. (How? Hold on, we'll get to practical suggestions soon.) The marriage bed can be "kept pure" when spouses are satisfied with each other and have no excuse to look elsewhere. Are you being the desirable wife your husband needs?

5. In this most intimate relationship we find something unique, something we often take for granted when life is good: Sex can be comforting. In 2 Samuel 12:24, after the death of their child, King David "comforted his wife Bathsheba, and he went to her and lay with her. She gave birth to a son, and they named him Solomon." Comfort, safety, protection, and a sense of peace can be found in the arms of a loving spouse. Because of his position as a human resources manager, Rich was required to lay off twenty-eight employees one day not long ago. That

night in bed, he pulled me close and in a moment of uncharacteristic vulnerability he allowed me to hold and love him.

Why Is Physical Intimacy Absent from Many Christian Marriages?

Kissing, touching, and many forms of exquisite physical pleasure are part of this thing called marriage. Without them, marriage is like any other relationship or friendship. Why, then, do so many husbands and wives act and feel like roommates, instead of lovers?

In one of my classes, we brainstormed a list of reasons sex is often our last priority. See if you agree with us. You may be able to think of more reasons, but here are a few: abuse (verbal, physical, sexual—past or present), adultery, anger, anxiety, children, communication problems, conflict, distorted thinking, distrust, fatigue, grief, hormonal imbalances, hurts, husband's disinterest, ignorance, inability to relax, inhibitions, lack of awareness, lack of exercise, lack of focus, moodiness, obesity, physical disabilities, pornography, poor health, poor self-perception, predictability, priorities, selfishness, seriousness (lack of playfulness), sin, stress, tension, time, tyranny of the urgent, unforgiveness, unfulfillment . . .

"OK," you say, "I've read the list and identified some reasons I don't have a great love life. But give me some specific information on why our society is so messed up when it comes to sex."

Since the beginning of time, we've been messing up the perfect gifts God has given us. We've complicated the issue of love. Here are some pertinent thoughts on the subject from Dr. Rosenau's *A Celebration of Sex.*

> *From boyhood on, men seem to tune in to sexuality more overtly and, in an unfair way, are regarded as the sexual experts. Girls are taught psychologically to control sexual impulses and do not tune in to sexuality as readily. The environment also takes a toll on sexual desire. In the midst of busyness and children, husbands often fear their wives could go days without sex being that much of a priority.[2]*

> *Women often struggle with relaxing control and abandoning themselves to pleasure. Some of this may be due to unfortunate double standards. The brunt of maintaining sexual control in*

dating relationships is placed on girls. God, in His sexual economy, makes both sexes respon-
sible for healthy boundaries. The unhappy truth is that so often boys try to score, and girls
slap hands and try to keep from getting taken advantage of, hurt, or pregnant. Wives can have
a difficult time releasing control and giving themselves permission to enjoy sexual pleasure,
even in a committed and loving marital relationship.[3]

Dr. Rosenau has a few suggestions on how to change our thinking to God's truth.

God gave each person responsibility for her own body and for learning to experience sexual
pleasure. But perhaps you are disappointed that lovemaking hasn't fallen into place as easily
as you expected. Don't be too hard on yourself. Take control of your sexuality and tune in to
cues more readily—for your pleasure and for your husband's. Give yourself permission to
have pleasure.[4]

Fantastic lovemaking is based on being a fantastic person. Attitudes are what count. True
sexiness and a fantastic sex life depend first upon being a mature, sexy person.

So you want to be the world's greatest lover? Build into your mind and heart the fol-
lowing character traits possessed by all great lovers: playfulness, love, knowledge, honesty, cre-
ative romance, and discipline. These guidelines, gleaned from the Bible, will lead to great sex.
Their effective use will show you how to truly arouse your mate's desire. Success is practically
guaranteed, but it will take some real effort to incorporate them into your life.[5]

JUST DO IT!

The bottom line is this: Obey God. Love your husband as God commands. "And his commands are not burdensome" (1 John 5:3). At some point, all of us must give up our own thoughts and reasoning, and agree with God, whether we like it or not. We must take Him at His word and obey Him, remembering that He never asks more of us than we can bear or He can supply (1 Corinthians 10:13). We need to "just do it," remembering that God promises He will reward faithfulness (and He's capable of blessing feelings too).

THE FRAMEWORK OF ACTIONS AND ATTITUDES

Not everyone's home is made from the same building materials. Look at your own life and ask God to help you decide on the most choice and appropriate supplies with which to build or rebuild your special relationship. Then work hard to put these things together with the cement of sincerity, the fasteners of forgiveness, and the girders of grace. Remember, the decorations (or feelings) come last.

You Can Rekindle the Romance in Your Marriage

Loving feelings don't happen by themselves. Feelings are most often the *result* of action, not the *cause* of appropriate behavior. God promises us peace, joy, and righteousness when we obey. Rarely can we be obedient without action.

Step One: From chapter 4 (Inventory Your Identity), bring your new understanding of your and your husband's personalities and love languages into this area of your lives. Remember that different is not wrong, and it doesn't have to be intimidating. Our differences can bring a richness and depth to otherwise ordinary lives. How can you make differences work for you? Know how you are different, and look for ways the differences enhance your marriage. Comment on and complement these special areas to your husband.

Step Two: Begin to behave like friends once again. Do you remember what your relationship was like when you first met and became friends? Here are some suggestions: Be positive and compliment him; consciously relax around him; keep it light (don't think or analyze too much); do fun things together; write notes of encouragement; give small, inexpensive, yet thoughtful gifts.

Step Three: Become lovers. To become lovers, you must continue to behave like friends. Gradually, add physical touch. Rub his back, his feet, and his body. Read up on what you don't understand about sex and/or talk to a friend, so you can be an informed lover. Become spontaneous, because we all need a good "wake-up call" and a little fun action in our otherwise routine, dutiful lives. (Yes, even melancholy people can nurture a bit of spontaneity in their lives, within given parameters.) Work on adding creativity and variety to your lives—"Spice it up!" Let me add one very important fact. Not everyone likes spicy dishes! Here in Lancaster County we love our bland "chicken pot pie," but occasionally I like a little Mexican or Chinese food—how about you? *God* created your desires and your tendencies to enjoy certain things more than others. Just don't pass up some of these suggestions because you've never tried them!

The Feelings That Follow "Decorate" the Relationship

God gives you a mind to believe the truth about love and sex—that they are good creations He designed for your procreation, productivity, pleasure, and protection. You are responsible to obey His command to love your husband by actively building love, honesty, knowledge, creativity, playfulness, and discipline into your life. Your sexy, loving actions and attitudes will be rewarded by the Lord as He provides feelings—love, delight, and desire—which bring pleasure and fulfillment to your marriage.

This sounds so idealistic. Any marriage is a relationship between two imperfect people; the marriage of two Christians adds God to the equation. How much each person trusts and obeys affects the success of the marriage. Can you make a difference by yourself, even if your mate is not doing his share of the trusting and obeying? Usually the answer is yes. However, your success will, of course, to some degree rely on the other person.

Not only are marriages between Christians and non-Christians potentially different, *every* relationship is different from the next one—because *all people are different*. Remember when working through this chapter and the next, God is your ultimate source of truth about what is right for you and your husband. He knows. And He knows best, because He created you . . . for love, sex, and pleasure.

I hope the following prayer is the cry of your heart. Take a moment to read it aloud to your heavenly Father.

Dear God:

As Your child, perfectly created by Your Master hand and designed for a beautiful love life with my husband, I give myself to You. I willfully give up to You every emotion, every expectation, every desire of my heart. I ask You to tear down the crumbling physical relationship I've allowed to decay and fall into disrepair. And I ask You now to re-create a strong, godly foundation on which You can help me build a temple of honor and pleasure for Your glory. Correct my thinking, and help me to put appropriate actions to this commitment.

I will obediently, by Your grace and courage, become the friend and lover my husband needs.

I will trust You for the feelings to go along with my new relationship.

Help me to love as You created me to love.

With love and appreciation,
Your loving and obedient daughter

20

Pursue the Passion

$\mathcal{D}$o any of these thoughts sound familiar?

- *"There are too many other things going on in our lives right now. Sex has lost its priority in our marriage—and I don't really think either of us misses it."*
- *"I am just so tired by the time I put the kids to bed, make lunches for the next day, feed the animals, and pick up the house, that sometimes I fall asleep even before my head actually hits the pillow."*
- *"We don't like the same things. We're opposites, even when it comes to sex. He likes it fast, spontaneous, and fun. I want to relax, take it slow, and connect with him."*
- *"If he'd do something around the house once in a while or add something valuable to our marriage, maybe then I'd feel like he deserves some good sex. Honestly, the man makes all these demands, and I do all the work. Where is the equality in our marriage?"*

- *"I'm too fat to even think about letting him see me without a billowy nightgown. Even when the room is dark, I can't stand the thought of him touching me and feeling the fat on my body."*
- *"I've never felt like I know enough about sex to do it right. So I just sort of get through it . . . as seldom as possible. If 'practice makes perfect,' I'm doomed to be a failure in this aspect of my marriage for the rest of my life."*
- *"I'd love to have sex with my husband more often, but isn't he the one who is supposed to be the aggressor? I don't want to come off like some wanton woman. I feel really silly, unnatural, and even ungodly when I want to pursue him."*

I didn't *learn* how to be truly passionate until years after the wedding! Many wives feel much the same. "Practice makes perfect" is a very good adage for the passionate side of marriage!

I dated several guys before Prince Charming came along. I treasure a few very special romantic experiences from my mid to late teens. One of my first and fondest recollections comes from going with a couple of friends to Hershey Park (we weren't quite old enough to drive, so our mothers dropped us off and picked us up). During that day in the park, my hand bumped my friend's hand and suddenly he had his fingers wrapped around mine. My heart melted on the spot, and I'm sure it wasn't the heat of that July day. He held my hand throughout the day and all the way home in the car. I can remember sitting in the backseat of his mom's car, wishing I could hit the "pause button" on my life and savor the moment. I'll treasure that feeling for my entire life.

My first kiss came from a shy boy I dated for months before he got up the nerve to kiss me. I will always remember the soft pressure of his lips on mine and the rush of emotion that overwhelmed my senses.

Back then, I was in love with the idea of being "in love." Many people call early love *infatuation*. Actually, I believe infatuation can be the beginning of love—the interest stage—but is hardly an over-and-done-with segment. Although love grows, blossoms, and matures, I still enjoy being infatuated with Rich.

A year or two after Rich and I started dating, he began putting three initials before his signature on a card or note, instead of the usual closing greeting "love." I will forever remember the day he explained Y.T.O.

means "You're the One." That's romance—knowing that you are the only one someone wants to love for the rest of his life. That's the ending of every romantic novel, movie script, love song, and sonnet—a forever love.

Romance contains the same ingredients I experience with Rich today —acceptance, love, and intimacy. But it hasn't always been like this. Dating, engagement, and the honeymoon were wonderful—full of anticipation, exploration, and fulfillment. Then the marriage began. Difficult situations, poor communication skills, daily stress, fatigue, overcommitment—they all took a toll on our relationship. The longer we were married, the less passionate our lives became. Not communicating well, we pulled apart, until there was a time I felt no romantic love for my husband.

My head knew I was committed to loving Rich, but my heart didn't feel it anymore. I didn't feel his acceptance. I didn't feel like he was actively loving *me.* We were about as intimate as a porcupine and a cactus. But God works in amazing ways in our lives—both for our good and for His glory. He adjusted my inward heart, and then my outward response to Rich was renewed passion. Today, our love life and romance is at an all-time high. Just the other day, I was working in my basement office when Rich came home from work. When I heard his footsteps in the kitchen above me, I felt a surge of emotion that caused me to scramble out of my desk chair, race at breakneck speed up the stairs, and throw myself into his arms as he entered the dining room. My delight in this miraculous scenario may sound silly to you, but in the light of the coldness, despair, and hopelessness I felt several years ago, this seems like heaven!

What happens to a couple's romance after the honeymoon, five children, insults, irritations, and wrinkles? Infatuation, intrigue, and passion seem to evaporate for many people. As a matter of fact, you have only to glance at magazine covers in supermarket aisles to see that almost everyone struggles with this dilemma.

The blissful state of *infatuation* does not have to disappear from your marriage. If infatuation means "to inspire with foolish love or affection," let me remind you that "there's no fool like an old fool." Love is fun. Love is silly. Love is glorious. Go ahead—enjoy each other! Anything is possible, and you can help it happen. Romance is not mystical, but a real need that can be realized in anyone's life.

Are you your husband's lover? You can be!
Let's take a look at the seven secrets of a truly passionate partner.

SECRET 1: SHE PUTS A HIGH PRIORITY ON ROMANCING HER HUSBAND

Many women sense their ongoing need for romance, but few realize they themselves can do something about it. Romance doesn't need to disappear with youth. Perhaps you've seen an older couple walking hand in hand and wished you and your husband could be more affectionate with each other. Yet you may have given up trying to resurrect your romantic life because you think it is impossible or you don't know how.

Romance is one soul touching another. It is not nearly so much what you do as how you do it, what you say as how you say it. Emotions, not the mind, are the primary stimulants—touched by romantic notions, words, and actions.

Beyond recognizing the need for romance, we need to dispel the mystery, ignorance, and stigmatism surrounding the word. Study romance and read what other couples do to bring romance into their marriages. Articles on the subject abound in women's magazines, and books fill bookstores and libraries. (You may wish to stick to reputable magazines and Christian authors!)

The truly passionate woman sees the need to romance her husband, and she commits to making this area of her married life a safe and stimulating environment for them both.

When is the last time you purposely aroused your husband, planned a romantic date, or enjoyed creative sex?

SECRET 2: SHE DE-STRESSES HER LIFE AND HOME

Feeling passionate is next to impossible in our modern world unless we figure out how to cope with things that threaten these positive emotions. Stress, the password of the day, is probably the number one enemy of romance. Added responsibilities, children, mental distractions, and fatigue all add up to a harried lifestyle. With little time left over to focus on enjoying our mates, weeks, months, and years can go by before we realize we've lost touch with each other—literally.

Most stress is directly related to overwork, poor prioritizing, and fatigue. You would not be reading this chapter if you didn't care about your marriage. Have you ever thought through the most basic priorities of your life? What is most important to you, second, third . . . ?

Now look at the things that fill your days. Are you spending the limited time you are given in proportion to what is of most importance to you? What can you do to get back to the basics? Maybe you need to rework your daily schedule. Maybe you need to build into your monthly schedule and budget things that will strengthen and build up your relationship with your man. Maybe you need to drop some responsibilities that compete with your marriage, even if they are otherwise important.

Remember to plan more time than you think you will need to prepare for passionate interludes. You will also need time to pamper yourself and relax, so you can give pleasure, instead of needing all of the attention. In a sense, this is not merely a part of your marriage, *romance* is knowing, loving, accepting, touching, affirming, and being one with that very special person who means the world to you (the one who *should* mean the world to you). If you are not experiencing this type of romance in your relationship, you need to make the first move. And this may mean a severe change in your outside commitment level.

But what if my husband has a low-paying job, and I have to work outside the home, clean, cook, and care for the kids? There just isn't any time in our schedule for quiet interludes; and when we do sit down together for a few moments, one or both of us often falls asleep! What do we do? A woman in this situation may be wise to make a list of the gains and losses connected with her job, pray over the list, and discuss it with a wise older woman and/or her husband. Also, part of de-stressing involves accepting things you cannot change. A friend of mine is married to a man who operates his own business from their home. They've made it a practice to always pick up the phone when it rings. She tells me callers have often interrupted amorous moments in the bedroom. "I can choose to get stressed out by this nuisance, or I can look for humor in the situation and help my husband get back in the mood—after all, we can be thankful it's not a picture phone! If it's a non-essential call, instead of getting angry, I enjoy *bothering* my husband until he can't wait to end the call and get back to the *business* at hand."

Another aspect of de-stressing is cutting out and cutting down. What responsibilities, activities, and time-consuming *things* can you eliminate from your life? Can you say no more often? Should you limit the children's extracurricular activities (maybe for their sakes as well as your own)? Can you declutter your home, simplify your schedule, and remove a few fringe responsibilities from each week? Even too many *good* things can be bad.

The truly passionate wife de-stresses her life and home so she and her husband can focus on each other for quality bits of time here and there.

What are three things you can do to de-stress your life in this next week?

SECRET 3: SHE ACCEPTS AND APPRECIATES THE DIFFERENCES BETWEEN HERSELF AND HER HUSBAND

He likes a hard bed; she likes it soft. He's hot, but she likes several quilts. He needs space, but she's a snuggler! When Rich and I first got married, our night life was comical. Neither one of us had ever slept with anyone, but I was a natural cuddler. On any given night a spectator would have laughed to see us move around the bed. We would start on our respective sides. I would move over to Rich's side to snuggle. He would move closer to his edge. I would move over some more. He would lie on the edge. Here I come. He would get out of bed and go around to my side and get in. I would find him and it would start all over again in the opposite direction.

Over the years, I've tried very hard to give Rich his "space." In return, he snuggles with me when we first go to bed, and when I'm asleep, he gently pushes me back to my side of the bed. Hey, it works!

Regarding other differences, men often don't share the same definition or basic appreciation of the word *romance.* Stereotypically speaking, women are the romantics and men are the down-to-earth, practical purists. Beyond this difference, bedtimes often differ, causing us to miss each other coming or going (so much for the snuggling). And another area in which much tension lies is our choice and preference for different types of clothing. And the list of differences goes on.

A woman confided in her counselor that she and her husband disagreed radically on cleanliness. Her husband worked in a coal mine and was never bothered by "a little dirt." He did not bathe regularly, but when he got really dirty he'd take a shower (getting most of the dirt off on the towel while he was drying). For years she had worked on him until she finally had him "trained" to take his work clothes off in the garage (by the washing machine) before he came in and put on casual clothes for supper and the rest of the evening. Even at bedtime, he was rarely clean. Her ultimatum in bed was this: If you want sex, you take a shower.

The counselor's advice was interesting and effective. Because the woman and her husband did not see eye to eye on the matter of cleanliness, she was told how to help him get a clear picture of how she felt about the situation. That day after work, he walked into the house to find her covered from head to toe in flour, waiting for a kiss. You may laugh at this extreme illustration, but sometimes we need to provide our husbands with a wake-up call—gently, lovingly, and on a positive note.

If you and your husband have different expectations, ask yourself: Can I comply with his wishes? Remember that God honors a cheerful giver. Being different does not make one person wrong and the other right. But in a marriage, we should be unified in spirit, even if we are different in practice.

The truly passionate woman handles differences between herself and her husband with gracious, selfless love. Sometimes she gives in to his preferences, sometimes she lovingly woos him over to her way of thinking, and sometimes they mutually agree to disagree.

Another way to appreciate your husband is to "sense" the differences between you. Although this letter is extremely personal, I share it with you hoping you will revel in the beauty of physical differences between you and your man. Perhaps my letter to my husband will encourage you to write to yours.

Dear Love of My Life:

Did you know that touching you and being touched by you is far and away the most treasured part of my physical existence? I cannot describe what it feels like to be held in your arms, to be stroked, to be touched intimately. I love the feel of your hands and your mouth and your body on my body—anywhere, everywhere.

Your absolute maleness brings out my most intensely feminine responses. You are so much taller, and harder, and stronger than me. You are warm. I love to curl up against you, to draw comfort and protection from your nearness, strength, and warmth. Your total masculinity emphasizes the contrast between us. You smell and feel wonderfully different. Even your clothes have a different texture than mine.

I crave your kisses. From a peck on the cheek to making love to my mouth, that intimate response to each other seals us together. I love your moods that vary our lovemaking from gentle and slow to urgent and electrifying. Your touch makes me feel like the most beautiful woman in the world. No one could ever take your place in my life. No other body could ever compare with the planes and hollows and textures I love about yours.

Thank you for loving me. Thank you for allowing me to love your body—and you.

Your loving wife

SECRET 4: SHE SELFLESSLY SERVES HER HUSBAND

Are you fulfilling *his* romantic desires? If not, why? One reason could be selfishness—we're all guilty of it from time to time.

I could have been selfish several years ago when Rich asked me if I had any interest in wearing a thumb ring. No, I really wasn't interested, but I encouraged him to tell me what he was thinking. He considered thumb rings to be very sexy! So I went out and picked up an inexpensive gold band and stuck in on my thumb. Rich loved it (and admitted that he was surprised I would "go" for something young and trendy like that)!

My reward came a few weeks later on Christmas night. I knew he was saving my last present for just before we went to bed, but I couldn't imagine what it was. (OK, the thought of a negligee had run through my mind.) Once in bed, he produced a little box wrapped in gold paper. Inside the small black box was an even smaller velvet box, which contained a gold wedding band in a size large enough to fit my thumb! The best part was what he said as he looked at me lovingly. "They don't make 'thumb rings,' so I had to buy a wedding band—but if I had it to do over again, I'd marry you a thousand times." Now, that's romance! Quite a reward for meeting a simple desire of his heart.

I am not encouraging you to take part in some sort of bizarre or even questionable activity your husband may desire—there are times when a no is quite appropriate. But most of the time, a more adventurous spirit on a wife's part would be appreciated. You need to learn the art of *making love to your husband.*

The truly passionate woman finds delight and satisfaction in giving up her rights and meeting the needs of her mate.

Here's a potentially fun fact-finding adventure for you and your husband. Take turns filling in the following sentence starters. And based on *his* answers, what can you do to fulfill some of his desires?

When I think of intimacy and closeness, I _____.
My idea of romance is _____.
I feel the most sexual fulfillment when you _____.
I'd like to make love as often as _____.
You might be able to talk me into _____.
I'd love it if sometime you would _____.
I wish you would _____.

SECRET 5: SHE IS USUALLY CONFIDENT IN HER APPEARANCE AND IN HER ABILITY TO DRIVE HER HUSBAND WILD

Do you have a poor opinion of yourself? Few of us are 100 percent pleased with our appearance, and we all have days when we wonder what our mates ever saw in us.

Mildred just didn't seem interested in Martin anymore—at least that's what he thought, because she wasn't doing anything to improve herself. She was buying baggy clothes that didn't do anything for her figure. Maybe she was trying to hide it—but the glimpses he got now and then were still pretty appealing. Mind you, he wasn't about to look for greener pasture, but he did feel sort of like he was being put out to pasture. Without even realizing it, he'd developed an attitude of resignation and indifference. But as long as Mildred wasn't putting any effort into the picture, why should he go out of his way to do the nice little things he used to do for her? Well, maybe that's just how life goes. . . .

Mildred doesn't feel pretty, isn't acting pretty, and has evolved into an ugly wife with an bad attitude. Ever felt like Mildred? I know I have. For years, I wanted to look better than I did. I would stand in front of the mirror and bemoan my heavy thighs and bottom. I tried diets, exercise, and new clothing styles. I was always searching for ways to be a beautiful wife.

On a trip to Dorney Park's Wildwater Kingdom, Rich and I spent a whole day standing in lines, looking at swimsuit-clad people. It was fun to see all the different styles and colors, but I was depressingly self-conscious of the chubby little body in my own swimsuit. After we'd been talking about our preferences in swimming attire, I asked Rich, "Do you see anybody here who has a hairstyle you'd like to see on me?" After a bit of cajoling failed to get a response, I finally came up with another, more insightful question. "What did you like about the way I looked when we were in college together?" He totally surprised me when he said he'd liked my "perky" style.

Perky? Charming! I'd much rather have received adjectives like classy, beautiful, romantic. Perky, huh? After I got used to the word and pumped him a little more about which people had "perky" hair, he remembered a style his very chic older cousin wore at the time. Being classed with this infinitely lovely lady definitely improved my mood.

The truth is he's right. I am a perky person. And now I have a perky hairstyle that women envy, I've allowed my wardrobe to showcase my "perkiness," and Rich enjoys my spunky attitude. I feel good about my appearance (even at forty pounds overweight), I know I'm pleasing my husband, and I am enjoying being me!

You may need to ask your husband the same question I asked Rich, and probe for fresh insights into who he thinks you are and what he loves about you. He may not know at first how to articulate his thoughts— and he will most likely not want to say anything, rather than say something wrong. But if you are gracious and sincere, he may discuss his feelings and desires with you. Taking his suggestions to heart will reap great rewards.

But what if you don't *feel* beautiful? If you don't feel beautiful, you won't act beautiful, and he won't have any reason to see you as beautiful. You can do something to help yourself feel attractive immediately. Go have a massage, manicure, and hairstyling. Buy a beautiful, silky, sexy nightgown in a large enough size to feel comfortable. Start awakening your own senses by wearing a subtle perfume. Although these things may feel intimidating and uncomfortable at first, the reward is well worth the investment in the "you" you want your husband to desire. If you are very insecure about this step, enlist the encouragement of a pushy but trustworthy friend!

Another quick tip to help you feel more sexy is exercise. Getting yourself moving helps you tone your body, and it also increases your sex drive. Try something easy and motivating that you can work into your schedule permanently—and increase your overall health.

Listen to Solomon's words to his wife in Song of Songs 4:9–11,

You have stolen my heart, my sister, my bride; you have stolen my heart with one glance of your eyes, with one jewel of your necklace. How delightful is your love, my sister, my bride! How much more pleasing is your love than wine, and the fragrance of your perfume than any spice! Your lips drop sweetness as the honeycomb, my bride; milk and honey are under your tongue. The fragrance of your garments is like that of Lebanon.

A truly passionate partner capitalizes on her strengths and compensates for her weaknesses, accepting and enjoying herself as she has been created.

Try this. Stand naked in front of a full-length mirror and critique your assets and liabilities. Make two lists: "things I like about myself" and "things I'd like to change." Discuss your list of negatives with a close friend whom you feel comfortable asking for wise and godly advice. Ask her to help you determine if there is anything on the list that can be changed successfully with reasonable time, effort, money—and how to go about it. Make a plan, write it down, and improve what you can, as you can. Things you don't like and cannot change need to be prayerfully ignored—while you concentrate your efforts and feel great about the things you *do* like about yourself.

SECRET 6: SHE MINIMIZES
THE FEAR OF REJECTION OR FAILURE

Many women live in fear. One woman fears her husband is going to look for someone else, someone more thin and attractive, someone with different measurements and a few less years to her credit. Another woman fears she will lose her husband to his work and hobbies, absorbing himself into another world—one that she is not a part of. These kinds of fear are paralyzing.

Have you ever planned a special dinner for yourself and your husband? You work hard to make every detail perfect, and you try hard to please him. At the same time, you are wondering if anything will go wrong. Sure enough, he's a little late, and the steaks are overcooked and tough. By the time he comes in the door, you are tied in emotional knots. The dinner is great, but you are in a distracted, uptight mood. Neither of you relaxes, and you can't enjoy this specially prepared evening.

Franklin Roosevelt told the American people during World War II, "The only thing we have to fear is fear itself." The truth is fear incapacitates us. It turns our attention inward to our insufficiencies and inadequacies. To be affectionate, loving, and sensitive, we need to focus on the other person and keep our minds filled with positive thoughts about how to please him. Second Timothy 1:7 says, "God did not give us a spirit of timidity [fear], but a spirit of power, of love and of self-discipline [a sound mind]."

As a vocal instructor, I'm tuned in to the masses of people who say, "I can't sing." Are you aware that only a fraction of a percent of all people truly cannot sing because they are tone-deaf? Fear of failure, most often deposited in a child's mind at an early age, causes the body to tense when singing. The singing voice is produced by sensitive musculature in the throat that needs complete freedom to "flutter," causing sound waves to wing their way through resonators, past articulators, and into the world. Even the slightest tension or "grabbing" of that mechanism in the throat can cause the sound to lose its natural beauty, to sound pushed, or to stop altogether.

Similarly, our beautifully complex human body functions much better under conditions of freedom, rather than duress, tension, or stress. Our mental person affects our physical person much more often than we realize. The solution is simply to relax, trust the instrument, and trust the One who made it.

Beyond fear of failure is fear of the unknown. Many women share a common problem—they don't know enough about sex to feel really comfortable with the whole topic, and they don't know whom to ask. Many excellent books by Christian authors are available as sources of information and comfort. Don't put it off any longer. Find out all you can about God's incredible creation of intimate male-female love. God knows all about sex. Ask Him to teach you.

Is it possible to learn to love your husband all over again—I mean really *love* him? God restored my lost love for Rich more than a hundred-fold. He is the God of the impossible. You can put your trust in Him. In return, He offers power, love, and a sound mind!

A truly passionate wife finds her completeness in God's approval.

What are your fears? Tell God about them, and commit to memory 2 Timothy 1:7.

SECRET 7: SHE MAKES HERSELF IRRESISTIBLE TO HER HUSBAND

Webster says *irresistible* means "too fascinating to be withstood." Do you fascinate or frustrate your husband? How can you turn his switch from "off" back to "on"? Remember that men are turned on by sight, while women are more motivated by touch. Look at your bedroom through your husband's eyes. Even if he appears not to care, a change of scenery, for both the room and for you, may be in order.

"But you don't know the real Barry," a friend told me. "He's busy, impersonal, and unemotional . . . a human android. To him, romance means sex, short and to the point. And when he is so unloving towards me, I can hardly bear his touch. Sex hurts and makes me miserable—and I know my reactions increase the emotional distance between us. I can't overcome this. I just emotionally ignore this aspect of my life. True romance is gone forever."

Several months later, I saw this same friend and her husband at a party—holding hands! Later that evening, she told me, "I feel like a new-lywed! I can hardly believe it myself. I redecorated our bedroom and lost fifteen pounds. Then I bought a beautiful black silk outfit and posed on our bed in front of our Polaroid camera. One morning, I put the photo in an envelope on Barry's truck seat. Later that day, he told me he couldn't keep his mind off me all day long. And it's only gotten better."

When Rich and I go out on a date, I often dress to turn him on. (We have a license!) Of course, I'm careful *not* to reveal anything inappropriate to the general public—he is the only one who knows what I have on underneath the clothes everyone else sees. I don't dress provocatively to attract the attention of other men, but to keep the attention and attentiveness of my husband and lover.

The truly passionate woman never gives up on a man, but makes herself irresistible to him. And in so doing, she guards her marriage and her love. Let me ask you again, *are you your husband's lover?*

Can you learn to become a passionate partner? The answer to that question is found in whether or not you value romance and will make the commitment to master the seven secrets of a truly passionate partner. We are not without help and encouragement, for with God all things are possible.

The question here is not can you plan a romantic escape for you and your husband, but *will you make it a priority and do it?*

A SPECIAL NOTE for those who have spouses who can't or won't:

Rarely do we hear someone address the issue of a husband who is not "hot" for sex. Yet, this situation is far more common than it appears.

The greatest reasons for the lack of sex drive in a man is *not* what most women think of first—"I'm ugly, so he can't stand me anymore." Generally speaking, a man's physical condition and his work/career situation are the two most common factors determining his desire for an intimate relationship with you. Sickness, injuries (even old ones that come back to cause pain from time to time), obesity, and other physical problems zap a man's physical-emotional state, just as they would yours. Also important are his overall concept of self and his necessary level of masculine ego. These can and will be positively or negatively affected to the degree he finds satisfaction, security, and recognition "on the job." A man struggling with job security, interpersonal co-worker problems, or an unfair employer (to name just a few possible problems) will most often find difficulty responding appropriately to you.

Maybe as many as half of the women I teach and counsel tell me they are the aggressors in the physical aspect of their marital relationship. One woman said, "It seems like I'm always the one to initiate sex. And I just can't relate when a friend complains about how often her husband wants it. Mine never comes after me. I'm beginning to get a complex. Is there something wrong with *me?*" Another woman said, "My husband just hasn't had the same energy level since his heart attack. Even though the doctor assures us he's fine, I'm afraid to start anything that might put him back in the hospital—or worse. He doesn't seem interested anyway."

No two situations are the same when it comes to relationships, even different aspects of the same relationship. You and your husband may have a good understanding about parenting but be miles apart on romance. Don't beat yourself up. Don't put pass or fail marks on yourself or your partner.

Pray for understanding to relate to your husband on his real need(s) level. Pray for patience. And trust the Lord to open your eyes and increase your compassion for your husband, even as God helps you to find ways to effectively minister to him on a physical level.

Sometimes, this problem seems insurmountable. You've tried everything, or you are too nervous to say anything . . . but the situation is affecting your marriage. Linda Dillow and Lorraine Pintus address this issue in their book, *Intimate Issues,* and share a letter written by the wife of a disinterested husband.

Dear Toby,

I am writing you because I love you and want our marriage to be the best it can be. I want to become the wife you need. I've tried many times to express to you in person what I'm feeling inside and it seems we always end up arguing, so I'm going to try writing this letter. I realize it is difficult for both of us to talk about these things. I really don't know why you've lost interest in me sexually, but I want to understand. I know I don't have a perfect body, but I'm not unattractive either. I'm scared, Toby, because I feel like our sexual relationship (really the lack of it) is changing the way we relate to each other. I feel unloved, unattractive, undesirable, and very vulnerable. A man complimented me at church Sunday, and I've thought about him all week. Please, will you talk to me and go with me for help? I want our marriage to work![1]

You've searched God's heart on the issue, you've done everything in your power to correct the situation, and you've tried to communicate the need to your husband. In moments like this the only response is to realize the problem is *his,* not yours. Fix your sights on God rather than your hurt. Fix your thoughts on the good rather than what is not right. Even though your situation may not change, your heart can be soothed and rest in peace.

Always accentuate the positive.

> *Dear God of Love,*
> *Grant me a godly, beautiful passion for my husband. I release to*
> *You my fears and inhibitions—thank You for the gifts of love,*
> *power, and a sound mind.*

·❊Conclusion❊·

Focus on
Forever

"*M*y mom and I were talking about your book, Nancy. We were wondering if you've got the guts to put a chapter in there that talks about what happens when nothing works." Faith sat at the other end of the couch, sipping hot tea, a challenge in her eyes. She and her mother, Grace, both suffered abusive marriages. Faith's husband divorced her (and the church he had pastored), and Grace had suffered for years at the hand of a tyrant.

In surrendered obedience and submission, these two women had lived with selfish, irresponsible, and abusive mates. Certainly these women had moments when they rebelled at the pain, chafed at the erosion of their dreams, and asked God "why me?" Surely from time to time they failed to see things from God's perspective and lean completely on Him. But they stayed faithful.

Faith's husband was truly self-consumed and, after less than ten years of marriage, he divorced her to lead a life of self-fulfillment. Could she have followed the teaching of God's truth and the practical advice in this book, met all her husband's basic needs, and still lost him? Most certainly, but regrettably, the answer is yes. Remember that marriage is a connection between two people. *He* chose to let go, and even though she did not, she could not stop the separation.

Grace, too, was unable to change her husband. She experienced rejection, humiliation, blame, and other abuse as her husband vented his anger and frustration, caused by living a life of sin. Yes, she prayed. Things did not change until her husband passed away. Slowly her emotional well-being and contentment returned, and she learned to enjoy all over again the simple beauties of life she had been denied for so long.

Even when your actions are good and your attitudes are pure, you can still be faced with pain . . . pain that doesn't go away. Perhaps, despite how hard you try to do your part to fulfill your goals, your husband lets down his end of the bargain. How do you keep going? Are there other options?

The world would like us to think that divorce is an option. We do not have space here to fully explore the subject of divorce, but suffice it to say divorce is not God's first choice for His children. Divorce is an undesirable end to one set of problems and the beginning of another. (If you are seeking a divorce now or suffering consequences of a past divorce, God still loves you. However, the mental, emotional, social, physical, and spiritual consequences of a divorce must be worked through with godly counsel.)

A woman whose partner is abusive or cheating on her should get professional help immediately. In some such cases a step toward reconciliation may include a time of separation. Major considerations of this nature need the expertise of men and women trained with coping and mediation skills. Call upon God, and then look earnestly for a Christian counselor or pastor from whom you can find help.

A different kind of problem includes the husband who does not want to leave the marriage relationship, but neither does he want to correct his side of the connection. Perhaps he doesn't realize his inadequacies. Perhaps he knows and refuses to do anything about them. How do you live with this man? How do you keep on keeping on?

THE PARTY IS IN HEAVEN

Faith's life without her husband is filled with a full-time job, all the bill paying, housecleaning, laundry, school meetings, running to special events, church . . . to say nothing of being both mom and dad to her daughter. In addition, she lives with the constant reminder of her failed marriage when she must forfeit her little girl to her ex-husband for visitation rights.

Faith told me her secret for holding on. "I take each day the Lord gives me, one day at a time. And I've memorized and try to live out Hebrews 10:22–24, which says, 'Let us draw near to God with a sincere heart in full assurance of faith, having our hearts sprinkled to cleanse us from a guilty conscience and having our bodies washed with pure water. Let us hold unswervingly to the hope we profess, for he who promised is faithful. And let us consider how we may spur one another on toward love and good deeds.'"

Grace, Faith's mom, told me what made it possible for her to hang on in such a desperate situation for so long. "I realized that although I was not perfect, my husband's problems were his, not mine. I aimed to be responsible for *my* actions, as I came to the conclusion that God would only hold me responsible for me, not him. I made a commitment to cling to God, take everything to Him in prayer, and be the person He created me to be *in my current situation.* I began to see things from an eternal perspective. No, the situation never changed; if anything it got worse as the years went by. But I changed. Inside. God gave me incredible peace in the midst of the pain—as long as my eyes were focused on God instead of the discomfort of my situation."

During her difficult marriage, Grace exemplifies the teaching in I Peter 2:21–23; 3:1–2, 8–12 (NLT).

> *Christ, who suffered for you, is your example. Follow in his steps. He never sinned, and he never deceived anyone. He did not retaliate when he was insulted. When he suffered, he did not threaten to get even. He left his case in the hands of God, who always judges fairly. . . .*

In the same way, you wives must accept the authority of your husbands, even those who refuse to accept the Good News. Your godly lives will speak to them better than any words. They will be won over by watching your pure, godly behavior. . . .

Finally, all of you should be of one mind, full of sympathy toward each other, loving one another with tender hearts and humble minds. Don't repay evil for evil. Don't retaliate when people say unkind things about you. Instead, pay them back with a blessing. That is what God wants you to do, and he will bless you for it. For the Scriptures say, "If you want a happy life and good days, keep your tongue from speaking evil, and keep your lips from telling lies. Turn away from evil and do good. Work hard at living in peace with others. The eyes of the Lord watch over those who do right, and his ears are open to their prayers."

When all else fails, when there is no one left and nothing worth going on for—there is God. When I finally got to this point in my own marriage, I realized a great truth that saved my marriage and my life. While I carried on my own little pity party, I remember crying out to God and saying, "Why can't I just have a little fun? My whole life is in the pits—can't there just be a party now and then?"

Then God spoke this thought to my heart: *The party is coming! Heaven is far beyond what you can imagine, and there you will experience complete joy at all times. How long is eternity? In comparison, how long is your human life span? And just what is the purpose of this life . . . to have fun?*

I knew the answers to these questions. No, of course God didn't put us on earth simply to have fun (although we do a lot of that too). I reviewed what I'd grown up believing. God's purpose for me on this earth is to glorify Him and in so doing turn people's hearts toward Him. The greatest party will be in heaven! But, for now, my purpose here is to glorify and serve God.

That day, I realized that on earth it is my responsibility to glorify God in my every action *and reaction*, looking forward to the party in heaven. In actuality, the time I have to serve God is as the blink of an eye, when compared with eternity. Surely I can hold on and fulfill His will during the short period of time allotted to me on this earth! With new determination and renewed excitement I began to obey God. I loved my husband, regardless. I served the Lord, regardless. And I began to have fun. Remarkable!

THE TEMPTATIONS REMAIN

Wendy's goal has been to fix Ted. As she studied God's truths on marriage, she got excited about the practical application parts of the lessons. She even tried to practice being positive with Ted. But her marriage didn't change according to Wendy's timetable. She'd identified problems and created workable solutions. Things should be getting better, right?

Regardless of the future party, we live in the here and now. *In this present world we want to fix problems immediately and move on.* But we can't correct years of inappropriate behavior in the time it takes to read this book and write in a journal. The principles outlined here are lifelong commitments. They must become a way of life. As the old adage says, "Practice makes perfect." You may need to give yourself and your husband lots more time.

There is also a temptation to change our actions on the outside without adjusting our attitudes underneath. If a woman does many of the nice things suggested in these chapters but harbors bitterness, resentment, and ill will in her heart, she is merely using a different form of manipulation to her own benefit. We must examine our hearts and motives on a daily basis, always praying for God's help to live sincere, selfless lives.

Unfortunately for Wendy and Ted's marriage, Wendy never dealt with God over some of the core issues and needs in her own life. She completed external exercises in building up her relationship with Ted, but she never cracked the protective coating around her inner core to allow God access to her hard heart. Sadly, the external changes disappeared little by little, until Wendy reverted to the bitter, angry young woman she had become a few months into their marriage.

More than just a temptation, shifting perspectives are an inevitability in everyone's life. While reading this book, I hope you have shifted your thoughts and perspective so that you are looking at yourself and your marriage with God's vision. But there *will* be times in the future when you are tempted to slip back into old thought patterns. Guard your mind and heart by keeping tuned to God.

When we set our daily focus on God and eternal issues, all other aspects of our lives fall naturally into place. *God's expectations are the ones* we must meet, His vision is the one we must see, and His love is the one we must have, regardless of our circumstances.

The mind is a powerful and awesome instrument. It has many facets to its design, and it possesses potential beyond what we use or can even understand. The Bible reminds us that our enemy, Satan, is a knowledgeable and hungry foe. He will do anything within his power to turn us away from the truth. The most subtle movement from God's truth can completely skew our whole perspective of a situation.

Wrong thinking was the primary reason I went for counseling years ago. I knew my mind was messed up, but by that point I wasn't sure how to get it back on track. I told myself, even though I knew better, that if I was a very, very good Christian, Rich would come back to Christ. And I rationalized that if I did anything wrong it would turn him off further to the Christian life. Daily I lived under that mind-set, trying to be perfect, trying to meet his every need.

I knew I was wrong, but I needed to clearly be shown the way "home." The counselor not only corrected my thinking and helped me appreciate my individual strengths and weaknesses, but he also helped me in other areas of misguided and ignorant thinking. Reading and working through the *Search for Significance* workbook freed me to see myself as Jesus does. Yet another lesson included the abuser-victim-rescuer triangle, in which I learned that if I refused to be one of the points of the triangle, the whole thing collapses and is nullified. Rich could still irritate me, but I didn't have to wallow in a martyr complex. Amazing what a little tuning of the mind can do!

But only a year after my last session with the counselor, I realized I'd slipped back into some incorrect thinking patterns. Reviewing my notes from counseling helped to realign my thinking as I was reminded of God's truth on the various aspects of my life. I encourage you to keep your journal handy and refer back to your notes often, in order to maintain your new thought patterns and heart attitudes.

Remember these three steps to success.

The key is your mind—*learn God's truth.*

You can forget truth—*keep reviewing God's truth.*

Learning is a process—*keep persevering.*

The Holy Spirit, who lives within us, longs to fellowship with us and keep our minds tuned to the truth. He is available to protect, teach, and guide us in the light of truth. God is our light and our salvation. He is the hope of our hearts.

Which temptation is most difficult for you? Are you impatient to fix everything and move on? Are you trying to patch up surface problems, while you harbor real problems underneath? Have you made changes in the past, only to revert back to your old self a few months or years after the fact? What practical steps can you take to ensure success this time around? Do you need to grab an encourager who will hold you accountable once a month for a year or two? Do you need to reinforce the truth in your own life by teaching these materials to another woman who needs God's touch? Do not go on until you set up some "safety nets" to catch you when the going gets tough and you feel you may be falling. Go to your calendar and mark several "checkup" dates when you can review your notes and reevaluate your progress.

THE REWARD IS CERTAIN

We are looking forward to the day when God will say, "Well done, good and faithful servant!" But even now, on this earth, we can know that God is pleased with our faithful obedience when He gives us more opportunities to serve, more difficulties to handle, and more responsibilities in His kingdom work (Matthew 25:14–23).

And the rewards of learning His truths, applying them, and obeying His precepts go even further. Regardless of how the world views the *success* of your marriage—regardless of how well your marriage meets your own expectations—God will bless you for fulfilling His call to be a godly wife.

I've discovered that some of the nicest, gentlest, most godly women I know have some of the meanest, most selfish husbands! Yet, over the years of marriage to difficult men, these women have allowed God to use their heartaches and disappointments to shape them into beautiful women of God who are thoughtful and sensitive to others. They've become *better,* not *bitter.*

243

Even in humanly hopeless marriage situations, the "fully complete, lacking nothing" wife can focus on the Source of true hope and look forward to the real party in heaven, while she lives a victorious, godly life on this earth. God's Word encourages us not to lose heart, but to press on toward the eternal glory that far outweighs any worldly troubles. Remember that life is a series of ups and downs—a continual process of learning, relearning, and habitually applying God's truth. God can and will use our situations to scrape and chip away at our sinful habits, to make us fit for His use and His kingdom. God is an expert at turning ugliness into beauty. This is truly a marriage that has moved *beyond expectations.*

Continue to hope. "Therefore we do not lose heart. Though outwardly we are wasting away, yet inwardly we are being renewed day by day. For our light and momentary troubles are achieving for us an eternal glory that far outweighs them all. So we fix our eyes not on what is seen, but on what is unseen. For what is seen is temporary, but what is unseen is eternal" (2 Corinthians 4:16–18). Our hope is in God.

I hope the verses and passages of Scripture from this conclusion will live on in your heart and mind in the months and years ahead. It is God who works in us to accomplish His work. I will join you in heaven one day soon for our glorious party. Until then, take heart—we can trust *His* heart.

We know that not every story will have a "happy ending" here on earth. But let us have hope, with no expectations. Yes, hope in God—He is in the business of doing miracles! Praise the Lord and give Him glory.

As I close our time together, I want to share what I call a "reverse prayer," because it is from God to you, not from you to God.[1] I pray that you will accept God's words into your heart and be encouraged by our great God and Father.

Dearest Child,

I love you with an everlasting love. I created your inmost being and knit you together in your mother's womb. I know when you sit and when you rise, and I understand your thoughts before you think them. I know your words before they leave your mouth. Since the beginning of time, I've known what will happen to you each and every day of your whole life. Nothing can ever separate you from My love.

244

To keep you humble and connected to Me, I allow you to struggle with weaknesses and discomfort. My grace is sufficient for you, and the pain I allow gives you opportunity to glorify Me. Where you are weak, there My strength is most evident. This brings Me glory. And I will never test you beyond what you can bear—no, I will always provide a way for you to bear up under the stress and keep glorifying My name.

You did not choose Me, but I chose you and appointed you to bear lasting fruit in My name. For I purposefully crafted you to do the good works I prepared in advance for you to do.

Do not worry, dear one. I will strengthen you out of My glorious riches, through My Spirit in your inner being, as I dwell in your heart because of your faith. I give you My power and My love, which is wider, longer, higher, and deeper than you can fathom. And I desire to fill you to the fullest measure of My Spirit—who is at work in you.

Do not conform to the pattern of this world, but be transformed by the renewing of your mind. Then you will be able to test and approve what My will is—my good, pleasing, and perfect will. Use the gifts, talents, and abilities with which I've equipped you. Be shrewd as a snake and innocent as a dove. Resist Satan, standing firm in the faith, because you know your sisters around the world are undergoing the same kinds of suffering.

Be joyful always; pray continually; give thanks in all circumstances. And offer My genuine love to everyone in your life—especially to your husband. I will sanctify you through and through and keep your whole spirit, soul, and body blameless.

Trust Me to do immeasurably more than all you could ever ask Me or even imagine that I might do. And as you delight in My presence, I will mold not only what you say and do and think, but also your desires—which I will fill to overflowing. When it is time, I will take you out of this world to live with Me in My Father's home—which is where I am now, preparing a special place for you.

I am faithful—trust Me. I am love—love Me. I am your God—glorify Me in every thought and action.

I love you,
Your Heavenly Father

‑❉ ❉‑

*Additional
Resources*

*P*ersonality resources from CLASS Services (800) 433-6633;
www.classervices.com

Littauer, Florence. *Personality Plus: How to Understand Others by
    Understanding Yourself.* Grand Rapids: Revell, 1992.
Littauer, Florence, Marita Littauer, et al. *Getting Along with
    Almost Anybody: The Complete Personality Book.* Grand
    Rapids: Revell, 1998.
Littauer, Fred, and Florence Littauer. *After Every Wedding
    Comes a Marriage.* Eugene, Oreg.: Harvest House, 1997.
Personality Profiles. This popular test is available in a self-
    contained pamphlet format directly from CLASS.

Other Resources

Blackaby, Henry T., and Claude V. King. *Experiencing God.* Nashville: Broadman and Holman, 1998. (Workbook and devotional also available.)

Dillow, Linda, and Lorraine Pintus. *Intimate Issues.* Colorado Springs: Waterbrook, 1999.

Downs, Tim, and Joy Downs. *The Seven Conflicts: Resolving the Most Common Disagreements in Marriage.* Chicago: Moody, 2003.

McGee, Robert S. *Search for Significance.* Nashville: Word, 1998.

Rosenau, Douglas E. *A Celebration of Sex.* Nashville: Nelson, 1994.

Vernick, Leslie. *How to Act Right When Your Spouse Acts Wrong.* Colorado Springs: Waterbrook, 2001.

Contact Nancy through her Website
www.hope4hearts.net
or by writing to
P.O. Box 10062
Lancaster, PA 17605-0062

Notes

Chapter 4: Inventory Your Identity

1. The material on the personality types is based on information in Florence Littauer, *Personality Plus* (Grand Rapids: Revell, 1983).
2. Littauer, *Personality Plus*, 162.
3. Gary Chapman, *The Five Love Languages* (Chicago: Northfield, 1995), 15.

Chapter 6: Forget the Fairy Tales

1. *People Weekly*, Special Collector's Issue Tribute (Fall 1997), 24.
2. Henry T. and Richard Blackaby, *Experiencing God Day-by-Day* (Nashville: Life-Way, 1990), 316.

Chapter 8: Accept God's Approval

1. The lies that follow are based on material in Robert S. McGee, *Search for Significance* (Nashville: Word, 1998).

Chapter 13: Get Through Grief

1. Carol Fitzpatrick, *Get a Grip on Grief* (Uhrichsville, Ohio: Barbour, 1997), 8.

Chapter 16: Resolve to Respect

1. James Dobson, *Love Must Be Tough* (Waco, Tex.: Word, 1983), 44–45.

Chapter 17: Speak with Sincerity

1. Ruth N. Koch and Kenneth C. Haugk, *Speaking the Truth in Love: How to Be an Assertive Christian* (St. Louis, Mo.: Stephen Ministries, 1992), 23.

Chapter 18: Stand Your Ground

1. Willard F. Harley Jr., *Give and Take: The Secret of Marital Compatibility* (Grand Rapids: Revell, 1996), 45.
2. Ibid.
3. Ruth N. Koch and Kenneth C. Haugk, *Speaking the Truth in Love: How to Be an Assertive Christian* (St. Louis, Mo.: Stephen Ministries, 1992), 26.
4. Ibid., 24–25.
5. Charles R. Swindoll, *Strengthening Your Grip* (Waco, Tex.: Word, 1982), 205–7.
6. Koch and Haugk, *Speaking the Truth in Love,* 199–200.

Chapter 19: Rekindle the Romance

1. Douglas E. Rosenau, *A Celebration of Sex* (Nashville: Nelson, 1994), 273.
2. Ibid., 192.
3. Ibid., 191.
4. Ibid., 192.
5. Ibid., 25.

Chapter 20: Pursue the Passion

1. Linda Dillow and Lorraine Pintus, *Intimate Issues* (Colorado Springs: Waterbrook, 1999), 123.

Conclusion: Focus on Forever

1. Based on Jeremiah 31:3; Psalm 139:2, 4, 13, 16; Romans 8:39; 2 Corinthians 12:7–10; I Corinthians 10:13; John 15:16; Ephesians 2:10; 3:16–19; Romans 12:2; Matthew 10:16; I Peter 5:9; I Thessalonians 5:16–18, 23; Ephesians 3:20; Psalm 34:7; John 14:2–3.

SINCE 1894, Moody Publishers has been dedicated to equip and motivate people to advance the cause of Christ by publishing evangelical Christian literature and other media for all ages, around the world. Because we are a ministry of the Moody Bible Institute of Chicago, a portion of the proceeds from the sale of this book go to train the next generation of Christian leaders.

If we may serve you in any way in your spiritual journey toward understanding Christ and the Christian life, please contact us at www.moodypublishers.com.

"All Scripture is God-breathed and is useful for teaching, rebuking, correcting and training in righteousness, so that the man of God may be thoroughly equipped for every good work."
—2 TIMOTHY 3:16, 17

MOODY
PUBLISHERS

THE NAME YOU CAN TRUST®

Beyond Expectations Team

ACQUIRING EDITOR:
Elsa Mazon

COPY EDITOR:
Cheryl Dunlop

BACK COVER COPY:
Julie-Allyson Ieron, Joy Media

COVER DESIGN:
Ragont Design

INTERIOR DESIGN:
Ragont Design

PRINTING AND BINDING:
Versa Press Incorporated

The typeface for the text of this book is
Centaur MT

93151